VIRTUAL ADDICTION

Help for Netheads, Cyberfreaks, and Those Who Love Them

DAVID N. GREENFIELD, PH.D.

New Harbinger Publications, Inc.

Publisher's Note

This publication is designed to provide accurate and authoritative information in regard to the subject matter covered. It is sold with the understanding that the publisher is not engaged in rendering psychological, financial, legal, or other professional services. If expert assistance or counseling is needed, the services of a competent professional should be sought.

The stories and case examples that appear throughout this book represent a variety of sources, including composites of patients, e-mails, and interviewees. There are also many stories and descriptions that have largely been unaltered, with the exception of names and identifying information, in order to protect a person's privacy.

Distributed in the U.S.A. by Publishers Group West; in Canada by Raincoast Books; in Great Britain by Airlift Book Company, Ltd.; in South Africa by Real Books, Ltd.; in Australia by Boobook; and in New Zealand by Tandem Press.

Copyright © 1999 by David N. Greenfield, Ph.D., L.MFT, CEAP
New Harbinger Publications, Inc.
5674 Shattuck Avenue
Oakland, CA 94609

Cover design by Blue Design
Edited by Catharine Sutker

Library of Congress Catalog Card Number: 99-74374
ISBN 1-57224-172-1 Paperback

All Rights Reserved

Printed in the United States of America on recycled paper.

New Harbinger Publications' Website address: www.newharbinger.com

01   00   99

10   9   8   7   6   5   4   3   2   1

First printing

"As the phenomena of the Internet continues to explode and permeate every aspect of people's lives the concerns about misuse and overuse grow. Dr. Greenfield covers a variety of questions that online users may have about their Internet patterns and provides practical guidelines to help them ascertain whether they have a problem, and if so, steps they can take. This book is a must for those who fit this category, those questioning whether they do, and their loved ones."

> —Al Cooper, Ph.D., Clinical Director, San Jose Marital
> and Sexuality Centre and Training Coordinator,
> Counseling and Psychological Services, Cowell Student
> Health, Stanford University

"The power of the Internet combined with the seductive nature of cybersex presents a unique breeding ground for addictive behavior to flourish. Its imperative that our culture understand the importance of utilizing this new medium with balance and perspective in order to maximize the beneficial potential of cyberspace. Dr. Greenfield has presented us with an excellent and much-needed resource to help web surfers avoid Internet pitfalls as well as climb out of virtual addiction for those already cyber-trapped."

> —Donna Rice Hughes, author *of Kids Online: Protecting
> Your Children In Cyberspace,* Vice President of Enough
> Is Enough, and Commissioner for Child Online
> Protection Commission

"While recognizing and sharing his own need to keep his Internet and family life in balance, Dr. Greefield offers practical and therapeutic suggestions for how we can stop. Not only is this book a must-read for those feeling out-of-control and not knowing where to turn, but it should also be required reading for those about to log onto the Internet for the first time."

> —Rand Holman, MBA, Market Analyst & Researcher,
> freelance business & technology writer

Dedication

This book can only be dedicated to my loving and supportive family, beginning with my parents who gave me the opportunity for life, and especially to my mother, Thelma, who never stopped believing in me back at a time when it was pretty hard to do so. Most especially, I must dedicate this work to my wife and children, who endured the sacrifice of the days and nights of my absence and had to tolerate my sleep-deprived irritability, always loving me just the same. I dedicate this book to my loving wife Marci, who gently reminds me of what is *truly* important, and to my *incredible* children, Joshua and Jonathan, who continue to teach me the true essence of love and joy!

Contents

Acknowledgments

It wasn't until I began to write *Virtual Addiction* that I realized how much of a group effort creating a book actually is. There are many people to thank for their assistance in bringing this book from "virtual" to "real."

First and foremost I'd like to thank my wife and proof-reader, Dr. Marci Korwin. She willingly took on the impossible task of sharing her suggestions and criticisms of the early drafts of this manuscript with me. This took courage. Her skill as a technical editor has proven invaluable in helping me to convey what is in my heart and mind accurately. Without her help this book would be far less readable!

There are many others whom I wish to thank, including Janet Esposito, LCSW, for her enduring faith and optimism in my ability to accomplish this monumental task, and for her tenacity in holding me accountable during those early moments when this book was only a concept. I would like to thank Dr. Karen Steinberg for her early guidance in the development of my research survey, and Dr. Kathy Rivet for her nothing-less-than brilliant statistical analysis and data compilation. I wish to also note the assistance of Rose Pike, Judy Hucka, and Wayland Wasserman of ABCNEWS.com for their coordination of the online research that appeared on the ABCNEWS.com Web site. Also of note are Drew Henderson, who assisted me in preparing the initial online drafts of the Internet Addiction survey, and Dr. Randy Lee, of Cyber-insights, LLC who is the designer and webmaster for myVirtual-Addiction.com Web site.

I'd especially like to thank Dr. Kimberly Young for her encouragement, openness, and inspiration to undertake this new and exciting area of study; Dr. Alvin Cooper, who helped support me immeasurably with logistical and practical considerations; and Dr. Michael Schwarzchild, who offered many pointers when I was just getting started. Finally, I'd like to thank my acquisitions editor at New Harbinger Publications, Catharine Sutker, whose belief in this first-time author gave me the opportunity to bring this book to reality.

There are many people along the way who have touched the process of creating this work. Some offered brief comments and suggestions, while others were more involved, but all have added to the depth and truth of these words. I am deeply grateful to those people I interviewed, surveyed, and received e-mail from. They freely offered the personal (and at times painful) stories of their trials and triumphs with the Internet. This book could not exist without their stories and would have no meaning without their courage to address their pain.

Introduction

When I first envisioned the idea for this book, it was based in part on my personal experience with the power of the Internet. I, like many of you, became almost instantly entranced by the online world. I noticed that I was spending far more time online than I had planned to each time (and still do). The Internet experience was exciting to me. It felt like an adventure, and it was fun. The *color*, *sound*, and *information*, all available *twenty-four hours a day*, felt almost intoxicating. The thrill of being online far surpassed my previous computer activities, such as word processing, desktop publishing, and financial programs. These typical computer endeavors never excited me the way being online did.

My relationship to the computer became more intense—there was so much more to *do* online. I was no longer limited by what software I happened to have on hand. For the first time, my computer felt like an unlimited resource. It allowed me to extend my reach into many aspects of the world. And it was creative, as opposed to simply being a management tool. Beginning with buying a laptop computer, and then going online, seemed to break the constraints of functionality for me, truly piquing my interest in the cyberworld. Obviously, I wasn't alone. Millions of other people have found the Internet to be a new and exciting way of relating to the world. I later explored my interest further by conducting a large-scale, online study of Internet-use patterns.

A subgroup of us, however, likes the Internet so much that we become "stuck" online. And although many of you haven't become addicted, you may feel that you're using the Net too much and are searching for a way to moderate your use. Still others of you are not sure what all the fuss is but are curious to know what the Internet is all about! You may be a parent who wants to learn more so you can keep up with your eight-year-old who's learning about the computer and the Internet. This book should be useful to all of you, as it contains an overview of the Internet, tools for recognizing whether or not you've become "stuck," ways to protect your child, and techniques for overcoming various, but common, Internet-related abuse problems at home and at work.

I am not against the Internet. I've received many e-mails from people complaining about my research, assuming that I disapprove of the Internet. Nothing is further from the truth. I like the Internet, and I'm fascinated by it. As a psychologist and a researcher, I'm interested in how it works and what contributes to its attractiveness for people, along with what makes the Internet potentially addictive. Because I see it as a fundamental shift in the way we exchange information and communicate, I believe it's important to understand the human-machine interface that we see with the Internet.

The Internet represents a significant departure from previous communications technology because of its universality and applicability to so many areas of living. It is both a new language, and a new way to communicate that language. It is both technical, and at the same time, personal. The Internet has applications in virtually every area of business and commerce, and I believe is poised to revolutionize many aspects of the world's economy. It not only serves as a new means to conduct business, but is *creating business* as well. I don't believe I'm overstating the relative impact of the Internet on the world when I call it the spearhead of the digital industrial revolution.

Who Should Read This Book

This book can be helpful to several audiences. First and perhaps foremost, *Virtual Addiction* serves as a self-help book for those of you who've found that you've become *too connected* to the Internet. You may find yourself spending too much time online, or that the Internet is beginning to interfere with your life in some way. This book contains information, along with numerous tools to offer education, guidance, and suggestions as to how to regain control of your Internet use. You will learn to develop some balance in your life. And you can learn how to respect the *power* and *usefulness* of technology, while *not becoming consumed* by it.

Virtual Addiction also provides a general introduction to what the Internet is and why it's so popular. This can be especially useful for parents of children of the digital age. Perhaps you still recall using typewriters, and may yourself be computer and Internet phobic. This book can serve as a helpful guide of the *do's* and *don'ts* of Internet use in order to avoid the pitfalls of Internet abuse and addiction. It can also educate you on how to be proactive in addressing this new technology. Knowledge of a potential problem can go a long way toward avoiding one to begin with.

This book can also be useful for employers, health professionals, human resource directors, corporate executives, business owners, and information technology specialists who utilize the Internet in their place of business. Because the Internet is most likely going to change the way we think of and conduct business, it will affect employees—including those who will become addicted to the Net. We *do* know that Net addicts are spending up to *one-third* of their online time at work! For Internet addicts, who conservatively represent 6 percent of Internet users, that can easily represent upwards of three hours per day online while at work *not* necessarily addressing work-related activities. Employers, as well as employees, need to better understand the Internet, along with its potential problems, in order to help prevent Internet abuse and addiction problems in their place of business.

There are also those of you who use the Internet to shop, gamble, or buy stocks who will find this book of interest. Significant problems have come about as a result of compulsive online shopping and Internet-based gambling. And there are record numbers of you investing online and using margin accounts to do so. Chapter 5 contains strategies for avoiding problems with these compulsive online activities. Chapter 6 covers how the Internet can have a serious impact on your marriage or relationship.

And finally, if you are simply curious about the Internet and want to learn more about it, you will find this book informative as well. Information is provided about the history, development, uses, and future potential of the Internet, including exciting new applications and technologies that are on the horizon.

Do I Need to Read the Whole Book?

You do not have to read *Virtual Addiction* cover to cover or in chapter order to derive benefit. I have repeated the main points and concerns throughout the book so you can simply pick and choose those chapters that seem most relevant or of interest to you. Because many of you have different levels of technical knowledge of computers and the Internet, I've tried to stick to the key concepts. Obviously there are more technical books available, but the primary purpose of *this* book is to offer helpful skills for overcoming Internet abuse and addiction, along with general information about the Internet. I have also included summaries of my Internet research, which I frequently refer to throughout the text.

Real-time Living

I present this book from the biased perspective that health and well-being are more readily achieved through living a balanced existence. I realize that this may be an ideal, not easily achieved, but I believe this to be the best way to approach most of life's trials and opportunities. I call this more balanced (albeit ideal) approach in regard to the Internet *real-time living*. Real-time living means living in your reality; it is using the Internet (as well as other technologies) without allowing it to overwhelm your life, such that you *spend more time online than you do with real people!* Spending time on the Internet tends to pull you away from real-time living. The allure of cyberspace can have an almost magnetic effect, whereby remaining balanced and centered becomes nearly impossible. All technology makes the task of real-time living more difficult, but the Internet is perhaps the most powerful distraction yet! The very nature of the Internet, for some people, can create an almost obsessive-compulsive approach to using this technology, potentially creating more harm than good.

The Internet represents a new area of scientific inquiry, and as such, our knowledge is comprised more of what we *don't* know than of what we *do* know. This book is but another small step toward greater knowledge. I hope you enjoy reading it as much as I enjoyed writing it, and if it can be of help to you or your loved ones, then my mission is accomplished.

The Internet

How It Has Changed Your Life

*The only constant in the Universe is
the unending process of change.*

There are currently several hundred million people online worldwide. That number is growing by ten thousand new subscribers every day in the United States alone! Online service providers are multiplying steadily and attracting thousands of new subscribers, many of whom have never been comfortable with computers previously. Many of the hottest growth stocks today are names such as EBay, Microsoft, Yahoo, AOL, Dell, and Amazon.com, among dozens of others, and all of which are companies whose product or service involves the Internet. Dell Computer (one of the largest computer manufacturers in the world, and a pioneer in *electronic commerce* on the Web) reported $10 million of online sales a day in 1998, which is triple the sales from the year before.

Electronic commerce is finally beginning to turn a profit. Experts estimate that as many as 75 percent of Web-based businesses may become profitable by the year 2000, representing sales in excess of $41 billion by 2002, according to Jupiter Communications. Forrester Research estimates this figure is to reach $108 billion by the following year! By 2003 Forrester also expects *e-commerce* (electronic commerce) to reach $1.3 trillion, representing almost 9 percent of United States business trade; they also predict that figure could increase to 40 percent by 2006.

Most major businesses now must have a presence on the Web to remain competitive in today's market, with approximately 28 percent of retailers having an active e-commerce Web site. The World Wide Web (WWW) today is what the yellow pages were sixty years ago, and you have to be there to do business. The Web is changing how business is defined and conducted.

Clearly, the Internet is here to stay. A recent survey showed that 45 million computers accessed the Internet regularly during early 1998, which represents a 143 percent increase over the previous two years. This geometric growth appears to show no signs of wavering. The Internet may represent one of the greatest developments in human communication since the advent of the telephone, and will undoubtedly reshape the way we live our lives for the coming millenium. The changes we'll see in the future are likely to dwarf our present technological marvels in a relatively short time. We're on the forward edge of the digital communication revolution.

World Wide What?

Perhaps we should talk about what exactly the Internet is before we discuss its impact on your life. The Internet isn't actually a thing. It is not a big computer hidden beneath a mountain somewhere. It isn't even a place with an exact location. Perhaps AOL (America Online) describes it best when they define the Internet as *a global network of computers that connects more than fifty million people* in more than *one hundred countries* around the world. The Internet allows for information to be sent and received at the speed of light with relative ease. This is the digital communication for the new age.

The *World Wide Web* (WWW), commonly referred to as the Web, is the popular multimedia branch of the Internet— where users can view not just text, but also graphics, sound, and video, and also quickly connect (*hyperlink*) to other media or documents. It's attractive because the Web works with point-and-click simplicity, and takes no special training to master. As with the rest of the Internet, people can use the Web to locate, read, and download documents stored on computer systems (servers) around the world. On the Web, however, the documents are presented as a series of *pages* (commonly known as *Web* or *home pages*) that are linked together to form a complete Web site. When you log onto these sites you can gain access to all of the information on the site and save or print it for your later use.

The Internet is not as new as one might think. Its origins reach back to 1969 with a military network called ARPA net (Advanced Research Projects Agency Network), which was part of the Department of Defense (DOD). J.C.R. Licklider, a computer expert who worked at ARPA, actually conceived the idea for the Internet, which he called "an experimental network of multi-access computers." He even seemed to predict, with uncanny accuracy, the tremendous popularity of the Internet. The "network" was initially only open to the military, followed by civilian users, such as universities and companies doing defense-related research, as early as the 1970s. The Internet truly began to flourish, however, in the late 1980s when most universities and many businesses around the world came online.

In 1989, Tim Berners-Lee, a British-born computer scientist, proposed the World Wide Web project while working at CERN (European Laboratory for Particle Physics) in Geneva.

The project was the predecessor to the modern Web of today. It was an enormous success and the project is credited with, in practical terms, bringing the Internet to the masses. Finally, the Internet was no longer reserved to DOD employees and university researchers. In 1991, when commercial providers were first permitted to sell Internet connections to individuals, usage of the network exploded and began the current growth trend. These initial commercial providers were the predecessors of today's Internet Service Providers or ISPs. Millions of new users came on within months, and a new era of computer communications began. By 1994 the Internet was in full swing and on its way to becoming part of the popular culture. The rest is history, with the growth of Internet-based computing outpacing the growth patterns of other home-entertainment technologies, including the VCR and CD player.

What's All the Fuss about?

Why is everyone talking about the Internet? Since I first began researching and writing about the Internet, there has been a virtual explosion of interest in the Internet by the mass media. The Internet has fully made its way into popular culture and is explored in almost every national magazine and local newspaper. You cannot go a week without hearing some reference to the Internet. Right now, with the Internet in its infancy, we've only seen the tip of this virtual iceberg in terms of its impact on our lives. Combine this growth with the phenomenal economic performance of new Internet-related businesses, and you have a socio-technological revolution with powerful economic implications.

Initially, specialty interests such as consumer products and services largely drove the Internet. *Adult Web sites*, Web sites that feature sexually-related material, were especially popular from the very beginning (and they are still). Some people even credit the development of *e-commerce*, electronic commerce, to the explosive growth of adult Web sites! Few

Web sites, with the exception of the adult sites, generated a profit early on. This has gradually changed, to a point where other commercial applications of the Internet are fast becoming viable due to the rapid expansion of subscribers and better access technologies. There is a steady growth of applying Internet technologies to traditional businesses as well as the development of completely new and innovative businesses that use the Net as the cornerstone of their product or service. Just look at the popularity of Amazon.com or E-bay! Every day we hear of new Internet-based companies that are showing dramatic growth, and there appears to be no end to the possible opportunities.

A New Frontier

The Internet is also big news. It offers the excitement of a new frontier, with new possible business territories to be conquered. It seems to capture our innate curiosity and thirst for new knowledge, along with our hopes and dreams of a better tomorrow. We love a new technology that offers a change for us. The Internet has breathed a new life into the overly technical aspects of computing and allows anyone with a computer and a modem to easily access the world. One enthusiastic user is quick to point out the obvious benefits of the Internet, which he believes have escaped me. His passion is not unique. The Internet does seem to bring about strong emotional responses from people, to almost fanatical proportions.

> *I believe Dr. Greenfield needs to spend some time in a nonacademic environment as a participant, possibly selling cars or flipping burgers. He should read a few novels, particularly James Joyce's* Ulysses. *He might begin to learn the context of the Internet, and something about the expansive magnificence of human cognition, and gain awe of man's hunger for experience and information.*

Companies such as America Online (AOL), Netscape, Oracle, Yahoo, AT&T, Sun Microsystems, and Microsoft are striving to popularize and commercialize this new communications medium. After all, this is a technology for the masses—a highly consumable form of *infotainment*. There's no doubt that the Internet is fast becoming a popular form of consumer technology, just like TV, CDs, and cellular phones, and it has a potential for similar advertising revenues. This possibility is not lost on the movers and shakers of the online world. There is considerable competition for control of the *Internet portals,* which are the entrance ramps to the information superhighway. Just as highway entrance ramps have signs and billboards, Internet portals allow for a great many people to "pass by" an advertising banner, perhaps clicking through to shop.

All this may sound like a pretty extreme way to describe a bunch of computers talking to each other! Because that bunch of computers allows people to communicate with each other at the speed of light, we're talking about much more. Where else can you, with the click of a button, access most of the information in the world while you're still in your pajamas? Faster modem speeds, better graphics, and new Web sites make cybersurfing a consistently new adventure. Time of day, geographic location, and even financial boundaries no longer matter as computers and Internet access become more affordable. One self-confessed Internet addict described the Net as a way to travel the world for the less affluent; the Internet equalizes the economics that separate people. Everyone is equal online!

Some Positives and Negatives

The Net offers many things we hold near and dear:

- It's quick and easy to access.
- It's relatively inexpensive.
- It's available anytime, day and night.
- You can buy or download (information, products, photos, audio, and video) that may not be available elsewhere.

- You can shop for things, or invest, from the comfort of your home.
- It's intellectually stimulating.
- It can change your mood and make you feel good.
- You can communicate with friends, family, and for business.

The downsides of the Net may be:

- Sometimes you wait forever to download information.
- The Internet can still be a nightmare to navigate, even with the new and improved search engines.
- The increasing user traffic can slow the electronic highway to a virtual parking lot.
- There is plenty of annoying electronic junk mail, appropriately called *Spam* for its obvious lack of nutritional value (no offense to Spam lovers).
- Some people can become addicted.
- There is not currently adequate protection for children who are online.
- When you are online, you are *not* doing other important things.
- It can negatively affect marriages and relationships.

Children and the Net

As discussed in more detail in chapter 11, one of the more serious problems with the Internet is the ease with which children have access to unwanted material, including X-rated adult pictures and videos. This concern is even greater on the Internet than on TV. Here, children can access the same information as adults. The computer cannot reliably discern a child from an adult. There are programs, like Netnanny, Cybersitter, and Surfwatch that purport to screen Web sites for adult content, but due to American ingenuity, the cyberporn peddlers have devised ways around these electronic filters. They simply disguise the lead-in or headline text to appear innocuous, sometimes still carrying the implicit suggestions of sex.

Many times there are no obvious indications that the information may be pornographic. Children, and especially hormone-crazed adolescents, are particularly good at figuring out these coded invitations. In short, you need to monitor your child's use of the computer and the Internet. You will learn more about the steps you can take in later chapters, and there is no protection device as good as an interested and actively involved parent!

The Dark Side of Internet Use

One of the biggest problems with computers and the Internet is that people can become highly compulsive and addictive in their use of them. Internet and computer addiction poses serious social implications for a world glued to computer screens. There's the risk of increased social isolation and withdrawal, a possible increase in depression, family separation, marital problems, and reduced job performance (it's hard to do your job if you're spending four hours a day surfing the Net while at work) (Kraut, et al, 1999).

There are new studies indicating that heavy Internet use increases depression and social isolation. My research suggests a clear risk of cyberaffairs and real-time affairs the more you use the Internet. With all the wonders of this new medium, there are dark sides as well. In my recent study in conjunction with ABCNEWS.com, a survey of nearly eighteen thousand Internet users worldwide was conducted. In that sample, I found nearly 6 percent of participants met the criteria for a serious compulsive addictive problem as defined by an adaptation to criteria used for diagnosing compulsive gambling, with probably another 4 percent having mild to moderate problems.

Even if conservatively interpreted, we're talking about a sizable percentage of Internet users experiencing some sort of negative consequences in their lives. People experience relationship problems, work difficulties, and other negative life consequences. Although the research is based on self-reports, there is clear evidence that there are at least certain segments of the population who are susceptible to the addictive potential of heavy online use. I will expand on what these potentially addictive qualities are and why the Internet is so addictive in chapter 2.

Perhaps the best testimony to the power of the Internet is seen in the following enthusiastic comments of this confirmed Nethead. It's written to be humorous, but it is representative of attitudes about the Internet. His statements reflect the *time distortion* that often occurs while online. Nearly 50 percent of our survey respondents noted this loss of awareness of time passing while online. Interestingly this is a similar phenomenon to the one reported by heavy gamblers or TV users.

> *I'm trying to find out if I have a problem. I mean, I know I can stop any time I want. It's not like anyone is injured because I surf the Web a lot. But then there was the time that I was reading the latest at abcnews.com and thought I heard a distant rumbling. The Web site didn't say anything about an earthquake . . . so I continued reading. That's when the wall in front of me collapsed . . . I was still logged on. Apparently I didn't notice the fireman standing on the ladder at the hole in my wall . . . yelling something about flames or something, but I was still logged on. So when the meteor hit the fire engine I barely even noticed it traveling through the still intact wall next to me . . . still no interruption in my surfing. I then had a strange urge to visit nasa.gov and find out all about meteors. Even though my left arm was numb from the flames I was still able to type and I could still see the monitor through the smoke. Yeah, I like the Web, but it's not like I'm hurting anyone!*

Neither Good nor Bad

The issue is not whether the Internet is good or bad. The issue is *your use*, or pattern of behavior, with the Net. Since beginning my research, many people have strongly defended the Internet for all its virtues. At times this enthusiasm bordered on almost fanatic devotion. The degree of feelings expressed about the Internet was intense. I've received comments from users around the world telling me of the wonderful experiences that they've had with the Internet. Some seemed almost angry with me for questioning the Internet and looking into the psychological aspects of its use and abuse. The two following statements offer a flavor of the hundreds of similar comments about my research, which I received online. These statements definitively demonstrate that communication online fosters a sense of disinhibition and ease of self-expression.

Why are you labeling the Internet as such a bad place? You're taking a new environment and making it to be a bad thing. I've stated that I'm a misanthropic malcontent. I've debated for years a good way of leaving society, or at least the tactile one that we know, yet still be able to feed the desire for interaction and input. The Internet provides me with both things. Now, by your standards, I may be in need of psychological counseling. However, the wonders of anonymity online, coupled with the absence of aesthetic bias, would make anyone like me run to it. It's not an addiction, it's not an escape. It's a selectable way of life. I can see how you'd think it'd be addictive to those who don't desire it, however for me, it's a choice, not an involuntary response.

I don't have a story of addiction to share. I just wondered whether it had occurred to anyone involved in creating this survey that with minor rewording, a good two-thirds of these questions could apply just as well to, say, books. (Do you ever lose track of time while reading a book? Have you ever stayed up so late reading a book that it interfered with your work the next day? Have you ever woken up and felt a powerful urge to return to a book you'd been reading the night before? Have you ever been sorry to reach the end of a book? Upon finishing a book, do you often find yourself thinking of ways you might obtain more books?)

Such comments have an almost religious quality when described by true Netheads. The issue is not about enjoying the Net. It isn't even about losing track of time. The key factor that makes any behavior dangerous is when it has a negative impact on your life. I suppose if reading books interfered with your life to the point that you neglected other important areas, they could be considered an addiction. Although I receive a lot of criticism for bashing the Internet, nothing could be further from the truth. I love the Internet. I think it is one of the greatest frontiers in our modern world, and perhaps, next to genetic medicine, may have the most positive implications for our modern world. I find the newness, creativity, and opportunity to discover new worlds exciting. I also find it to be a powerfully alluring medium, sometimes keeping me logged-on much longer than I should have been.

The intensity of my interest in the Internet is caused in part by the power that it seems to exert in many people's lives. I do not see it as an inherently destructive force, but rather as a powerful medium that needs to be understood and respected. Also of interest is the significant impact that the Internet has, and will continue to have, on our society. For example, this college junior describes a typical experience of a Nethead.

> When I was a junior in college, my school got hooked to the Internet, and so did I. It started out just surfing the chat rooms. We only had three computers that had access to the Internet, and sometimes you had to wait hours, but I did. Slowly, I became addicted to chat rooms. I even developed a few online pen-pal relationships with people. It was harmless, right? Eventually, I started MUDDING [multiple user dungeons and dragons]. I was even more addicted. There was an appeal to it because the people I came to know were only a little over two hours away. Sometimes we'd even get in groups and hang out in Tuscaloosa, which was halfway for all of us. Sometimes I stayed on the Internet twenty hours a day. Right after class, I headed down to the computer lab. During the peak time of my addiction, the computer lab had all the computers with Internet access, so I didn't have to wait. I started failing

classes. I could get on the computer at noon, and not get off until eleven P.M. when the lab closed.

The potential social implications here are staggering. While the Internet can connect you to everyone in the world, it can simultaneously isolate you from those in your life. Herein lies the Internet paradox: *in order to expand your world, you have to nearly isolate yourself to do so.* Any revolution in the way we communicate is likely to have social and psychological implications. The fact that the Internet can be so addictive creates an even more powerful impact on both a personal and social level. Any technology that can isolate its user, such as the Internet, must have significant implications for our society. We are already seeing this with the way the Net has affected marriages. I've seen numerous couples who have had significant changes in their family as a direct result of the power of the Internet. Many people are neglecting major areas of their lives, including relationships, work, health, money, and so on.

The Net: A Pandora's Box for the Digital Age

How can something that is so mind-expanding also be so damaging? The answer may be in the way we currently access the Net. Right now we do so by logging on through a computer that is a discrete machine usually located in a separate room, away from people. This process automatically isolates you from others. This isolation is further intensified when you engage in private chat room discussion, online affairs, or cybersex. In addition, you typically need a phone line (unless you have a cable modem) and because many people use their main home phone line, this again continues to isolate you from others by preventing people from calling in.

In a few years, however, you probably won't have go off to the computer room to do your thing. Rather, you'll simply turn on your TV/Internet/telephone box and access the Web and TV simultaneously. Web TV is basically a small computer and modem hooked up to your TV so that you have access to the Internet on your television, without a computer. *Web TV* is an early iteration of what will eventually be the core of our home entertainment centers. Add this to other digitally based entertainment products such as DVD/DIVX, CD, digital cable, and satellite technology and your entertainment/communication system will likely become an integrated, digital system. DVD and DIVX are new digital video disc formats that allow for digital audio and video to be stored and played on your computer and home players. They represent the next generation of recorded video images, and are far superior to other formats, such as video tape and laser disc. Because the images are digitized, there is greater flexibility in what can be viewed. This new TV/computer is likely to be placed in more public places, such as a den or family room. The computer will no longer be a distinct complex part to be mystified by; rather it will be so seamlessly integrated with the Internet that it will resemble a TV in its relative simplicity and frequency of use.

The Power of the Net—Losing Your Balance

With the rapid growth of the Internet there are bound to be problems. Although there are no definitive numbers to date, it seems clear, that for some people, computer and Internet use can escalate to addictive proportions. Although the current research has been limited, there are now nearly a dozen studies that point to problems with compulsive Internet use. Many of these studies aren't controlled; they're either anecdotal or survey-based, which tends to dilute some of the generalizations that can be made about the results.

There is, however, enough clinical data from psychologists and other mental health professionals around the world to begin to develop some preliminary conclusions. There are also many friends and family members who report Internet addiction in a loved one. I've received countless e-mails and phone calls reporting horror stories from frustrated husbands and wives, who describe what appears to be Internet-addictive behavior. Based on the available research to date there may be nearly two million Internet addicts worldwide! I believe this number to be an understatement, due to Internet use growing larger at such rapid rates.

New Opportunities

There does appear to be limitless opportunity online. In business, education, healthcare, entertainment, and communications, the potential applications are almost endless. There will undoubtedly be continued growth of the Internet, and with this growth it's necessary that we develop a greater appreciation for the power that the Internet can yield. Many of you will become enamored only temporarily, and then resume reasonable use, but some of you will not. *Virtual Addiction* is for those of you who lose your balance. It is my hope that this book will educate and inform you of the power of the Internet, and help those of you who have become lost on the information superhighway to find your way home again, and to regain a sense of direction in your life.

The Nature of Addiction

Can You Be Addicted to a Computer or the Internet?

*Problems are simply old solutions
that no longer work.*

Her screen name is "Hot as Fire." She is HIV and Hepatitis B
positive and she works as a dominatrix in an S&M club in
New York City. This is a far cry from the homemaker with
three children Monique, her real name, was only a few short
years ago. Now she lives part-time in a small suburban town
with her estranged husband and children. The rest of the time
she is dressed in leather, beating men into submissive

satisfaction. Today, one of her greatest worries is how her HIV status affects her family, particularly her nine-year-old son. She says that if it weren't for him, she'd go public with the dangers of the Net. Financially ruined, and physically ill, Monique described her tragic story to me.

It all began with a gift from her husband for Christmas. Opening the big, colorful box that contained the new computer was the beginning of a strange new adventure. Monique had no idea what a computer was, let alone how to use it. She learned quickly. She soon discovered *bulletin boards* (places where information, resources, and friendships are shared, typically around a common theme or topic) and began to meet friends online. She realized that it didn't matter to her cyberfriends that she was overweight and insecure. She even discovered a chat room just for her; it was a room for BBWs (Big Beautiful Women) and it attracted overweight women and the men who might love them. It was a place of promise and acceptance. This was a place where Monique could be herself without being physically seen.

Soon Monique's self-esteem began to increase. Life began to take on more excitement and promise than her homemaking had given her. She still cared for her husband, three children, and two stepchildren, but she did "only the basics." She was too busy talking online. When she wasn't online, she started going out more and taking better care of herself. She began to lose weight, and started buying new clothes that made her feel attractive. Whereas previously she would deny her needs to take care of her children, she was now putting herself first (perhaps for the first time in her life). Initially, this might have been healthy, as she felt better about herself than she had in years. Her weight loss and her new cyberfriends began to fullfill her life. It all felt so good she never realized how compulsive she was becoming in using the Internet.

By now she was spending many hours a day online. Some days she spent more time online than off. Her phone and Internet bills totaled hundreds of dollars a month as she spent between eight and twelve hours a day online (this was in the early days of paying for Internet access by the hour). What started out as friendly chat room conversations soon became *cybersex*. Cybersex is consensual sex practiced by typing descriptions of sexual acts and exchanging a verbal dialogue via e-mail. Often masturbation is practiced while one is reading descriptions of imaginiary sexual acts being performed. Cybersex contains a lot of fantasy and does require some imagination, but many people report it to be a powerful and satisfying experience. Cybersex was soon followed by telephone sex. From there, it didn't take very long to reach the inevitable hotel meeting for "real-time" sex. These cyberlovers were all relative strangers, except for the time they spent "together" online.

At the suggestion of a cyberfriend, Monique soon found herself gravitating toward a B&D (bondage and discipline) room on the Net. This had been suggested to her by one of her new online friends. By this point, Monique was becoming well known and popular in her BBW room and she enjoyed her new "virtual status" and the attention she got from it. In the cyberworld she was moving up in the ranks. In her real world she was out of control. Internet use can quickly escalate to addictive proportions. When you're addicted to something, the addiction can become more important than family, friends, and work. Although cybersex is somewhat satisfying, many people take it from cybersex to the real world. Frequently there are phone calls, with phone sex often involved.

It took many more months and a lot more pain to bring Monique back to reality again. Unfortunately for her and her family, she brought back some all too real reminders of her trip into cyberspace. Monique had become addicted to the Internet. And the diseases she tragically contracted were far from "virtual."

Monique's story has a partially happy ending. She did recognize the negative effect the Internet was having on her life and took steps to begin to reclaim some parts of her life. There are some aspects of Monique's life that can never be the same, however.

Stories such as this are becoming a more familiar scenario reflecting the darker side of the Internet. This is a side that is far from the hopeful promise that this new electronic frontier proposes. It is one of many tragedies that reflect the powerfully addictive nature of online life for some people who lose their balance on the Internet. *Powerlessness* and *unmanageability* are two common effects of a prolonged addiction. And often people report being "out of control" of their behavior, almost as if the *addiction* takes precedent over their better judgment.

The Reality of Internet and Computer Addiction

Compulsive Internet use seems to produce the same type of *tolerance* and *withdrawal* as other addictions. There is also growing research supporting the conclusion that many Internet users, perhaps as many as 6 percent, are being negatively affected by their Internet use. It seems that you can develop a tolerance to Internet use. That is, you may need greater amounts of time online or to access more stimulating material. Although Web sites need not be sexual in nature in order to become addictive, they often are for a great number of Netheads. Of those who meet the criteria for Internet addiction, 62 percent regularly logged on to pornography sites, and reported experiencing sexual arousal while online "sometimes." They spent an average of over four hours per week viewing material on the adult sites, and 37.5 percent reported masturbating while online! For these Internet users, the Net offered a high degree of stimulation and sexual excitement.

Is It Physical or Psychological?

The distinction sometimes made by health professionals between physical and psychological addictions is probably irrelevant, and is certainly impractical. We are wholistic beings. After all, you don't see many bodies walking around without brains or vice versa do you? (Okay, maybe you know a few people who fit the bill!) This artificial distinction between the mind and body has little practical validity for understanding how addiction actually works, because our minds and bodies are actually integrated and function as one and the same.

There are distinct chemical pathways that connect virtually every part of the body to our central nervous system, including the endocrine system. In short, we are what we *think*, what we *feel*, and *do*. Everything we experience has an impact on our psychological and physical health and vice versa. Health, then, is the integration and appreciation of the interrelationship between *all* parts of us, including the less tangible spiritual side of ourselves. To follow, disease is the absence of that *healthy integration*, when one experiences a *dis-ease* in their life. Addiction can be a chief symptom for how that disharmony has become expressed in our lives.

The psychological dependence that occurs when someone becomes habituated (tolerant) to a behavior or substance is very powerful. You can develop strong rituals and habits around the behavior which become woven into the very fabric of your life. Almost all of the people I treat for an addiction feel a real *need* for the behavior or substance that controls them. And many of the people I have interviewed for this book state that they need their Internet use in much the same way. The Internet has become unmanageable for them and has taken a central, and dysfunctional, position in their life.

Perhaps no case better expresses the power of Internet addiction than Sandra Hacker's (yes, that really is her name!). She made front-page news as the first well-publicized legal case involving Internet addiction. She was charged with neglecting her children while spending all day and night online. She'd apparently left her children to live in squalor while she locked herself in a nice clean room with a new computer and modem. This case drew a lot of publicity because it broke the country's collective denial about the possibility of addiction to the Internet, and it showed how children can be negatively affected by the Internet. Sandra Hacker's story demonstrates that the power of Internet addiction can override even the most basic instincts, such as protecting our children. And while it does represent an extreme example, her case is probably less unique than we think. Since then, I have been contacted numerous times to consult with individuals about Internet addiction and child custody issues, along with cases where Internet addiction has affected marriages, jobs, finances, and relationships.

We Get High from What We Do

Behaviors that are potentially addictive include *work, sex, gambling, food, exercise, shopping, television, computers, the Internet, in addition to drugs and alcohol use*. This list is by no means exhaustive. There are probably as many possibilities as there are potential pleasures. The basic psychobiological process of addiction is fairly similar regardless of the initial source of the "high." What do all the above behaviors have in common? What makes them addictive? And why do some individuals become psychophysiologically dependent while others do not? After all, these are behaviors that *most* people engage in on a regular, if not daily, basis without any problems. However, when combined with certain circumstances, an addictive pattern can emerge.

This addictive pattern often isn't appreciated until the addiction has taken serious hold and there are obvious negative consequences. It's likely that many people become addicted to seemingly innocuous behaviors; the Internet is simply the most recent addition to a long list of behaviors that we may find addictive. In fact, a cable modem installer recently commented to me that he has never seen such strong reactions from people as when their Internet service is interrupted. He described a significant "withdrawal" from the Internet (as compared to TV) when their Internet access went down.

Losing Control

Fred's story reflects a fairly typical scenario of a man whose sexual preoccupation became dangerous when combined with the power of the Internet. Fred is a twenty-nine-year-old professional with a very promising career. His excessive, and at times, self-defeating Internet use pattern demonstrates how sexually addictive the Internet can be. Fred was exhibiting classic symptoms of powerlessness in his life. When he came to see me, he was virtually out of control.

Fred is on the corporate fast track to money, and success, and is contemplating becoming engaged to his girlfriend of three years. Everything seems great, except that Fred was addicted to pornography on the Internet. When I first met him, he was spending several hours during and after work viewing pornographic pictures, sometimes until three A.M. only to be at work again by seven A.M. He compulsively rented adult videos and planned his business trips around having access to the Net or to adult video stores. Sometimes he'd buy sexual products over the Net, and has even been ripped off through his credit card because of shopping online. Fred probably has a sexual addiction, with the Internet being used as a means to gratify his cravings. For Fred, any use of the Internet can easily trigger a relapse of his compulsive sexual behavior due to easy access of pornography online.

Fred spent hundreds of dollars on Internet access while surfing the Net for hours searching for naked women. He described himself as obsessed and out of control, but unable to stop on his own. He'd tried a half dozen times before, but with no lasting results. Fred finally came to see me after he saw our ad and Web site that discussed Internet addiction issues. He'd hit bottom. He no longer felt he had control of this part of his life and he was scared. He could control every other aspect of his life, but this one was too powerful to handle alone. Through psychotherapy and a therapy group he has been getting the help he needs, and his life is beginning to turn around. For Fred, and many others, any interaction with the Internet *can become* so sexually stimulating that it leads to an addictive pattern of use.

The Use and Abuse of the Internet

Why is the Internet so addictive? To answer this question, let's look for a moment at the nature of gambling which may have a lot in common with the Internet. Experts agree that gambling is potentially addictive for some people. There are many theories as to why gambling is addictive. It is likely to be a combination of the social aspects of gambling, along with increases in dopamine, adrenaline, and other neurochemicals that contribute to the addictive excitement of gambling. Just look at the presence of Gamblers Anonymous (GA), support groups for family members of gambling addicts (GAMANON), and the numerous programs sponsored by private and governmental agencies. Even state lottery commissions and casinos offer assistance! In Connecticut there are advertisements for help glued onto the lottery machines. Clearly, gambling addiction is a real phenomenon and there are those individuals who gamble well beyond their means, in a compulsive and self-destructive manner.

Gambling addictions seriously affect the quality of the addict's relationships and health. People have lost their houses, cars, families, and jobs, all the while continuing to gamble. They may be in a casino, betting on a sporting event, playing the stock market, lotto, or simply playing bingo—all for the purpose of receiving that "hit."

All of these behaviors can produce an elevation of the neurochemical *dopamine*. We experience dopamine as a sense of exhilaration. Although this process is short-lived, it is very intense, pleasurable, and habit forming. Most of us like to experience pleasurable things, and to stop unpleasant things. We will repeat experiences we see as pleasurable. Normal life seems dull compared to the excitement of the addiction "hit" and many addictions get their start from a general sense of boredom. Boredom can present you with an uncomfortable feeling, a sense of being ill at ease, which many of us try to escape from. I believe that many self-destructive behaviors get their start this way. They are initially an attempt to solve a problem (boredom), but in the process, an addiction develops, beginning a new problem.

We don't like to feel uncomfortable and we don't have time to feel bad. Feeling bad requires us to think, feel, and perhaps *do something* that might take some effort to change our life. This can be a hard thing for many of us to do. The reasons why this is so hard are complex. It probably involves an expectation in our culture that we *shouldn't* have to feel bad at *all*; and if we have to feel bad, it should *not be for very long*. Addictions may, in part, be the result of a society that has lost its ability to heal itself. A society with no tolerance for pain, and no patience to change. Addictions are a way of separating us from our inner experience and this is done with the implicit approval of everyone we meet, including the media. No one wants to *feel anything*, least of all, anything uncomfortable. So we go on and try to numb our discomfort in a variety of ways, with the Internet being the latest. That is not to say that the Internet is all bad; it certainly isn't. It will make a huge contribution toward improving the quality of our lives. However, the Internet's addiction potential is simply the opposite side of the positive coin and represents a dialectic of the good it can do.

The Longest River: Denial

A hallmark of someone who is engaging in an addiction pattern, but who hasn't accepted that their behavior is out of their control, is *denial*. Denial is a psychological defense mechanism that enables you to continue to engage in a behavior in spite of obvious negative consequences in your life. It's a way to protect yourself from seeing or feeling things that are unpleasant.

In the case of the gambling addict, there may be repeated warnings from his or her spouse that they will not tolerate continued spending of household savings, job loss, and constant harassment by creditors. In light of this, the gambling addict will still deny that they have a problem with gambling, believing that they have complete control over their actions. Denial permits you to distort reality, a very powerful psychological defense; it can have devastating consequences on your life. This ability to disregard such negative consequences while continuing the behavior is a hallmark of denial.

Denial is present, to some extent or another, in all addictions. It's necessary, in the development of an addictive process, to experience a sense of denial while the addiction is beginning to take hold. Otherwise people wouldn't continue with the addictive behaviors. Because of denial, the full effect of the negative behavior is never fully appreciated until the consequences become so overwhelming that they can no longer be ignored. This is sometimes referred to as *hitting bottom*. People may continue their behavior indefinitely, with no recognition of the negative consequences of their actions, in spite of numerous personal disasters.

Often an individual will not seek help for a specific problem, unless they've recognized that they're no longer in control of the situation and need help. This usually happens at a point when the negative results of their addiction have become grossly obvious and their denial is broken. It is a process that cannot be rushed. Each person has to discover their own time frame for how and when to deal with their addiction. This, of course, can be very frustrating for family and friends of the addict, who often notice the problem long before the addict does.

Negative consequences of Internet use vary considerably. I have been consulted on Internet cases where employees have been caught using their work computers for personal Internet access (in some cases wasting considerable company time and/or downloading sexually-related material onto their terminal). Individuals can actually be charged with sexual harassment as a consequence of exposing their co-workers to sexually explicit material. I've also seen numerous cases where couples came in with significant marital or relationship problems due to Internet abuse, at times even resulting in a child custody investigation.

Every day I hear stories of people getting into trouble with their online behavior. Our society, along with the mental health and addictions professions, is in collective denial about the extent of the real problems with the Internet. Few people, except for those who've had a problem, recognize the power and attraction of being online. Although it's probably not an epidemic, I have little doubt that millions of people are experiencing negative consequences in their lives because of their compulsive use of the Internet. And I believe the number of people affected will only continue to grow.

The Unique World of the Internet

There are many unique psychological characteristics of an Internet experience, some of which are also shared with gambling. What follows is a description of some of the psychological experiences reported by many people online. My research on Internet use and addiction (virtual-addiction.com) has supported the experience of many of these qualities, several of which appear to be universal qualities of Internet use.

An Online High—Stimulation

The Internet contains an incredible universe of information that is interesting, unique, and stimulating. Information is available about virtually (no pun intended) *any* topic area, including sexuality and all forms of imaginable adult entertainment. Currently the four most popular areas accessed on the Net are *financial information, sports, automobiles,* and *sex,* but this representation is changing even as this book goes to press. I believe that the Internet's spiraling growth was jump-started by sexually-related Web sites; it was the sex Web sites that seemed to be making money almost instantly.

The stimulating effect of the Internet is *not* only due to sexual material however. My research suggests that just the act of connecting to *a world of information* is intoxicating to many people. People report that the stimulation found on the Internet has the same intense, almost sexual excitement, they might experience in a casino.

Most people surveyed found the Internet to be intellectually stimulating at least "sometimes," and "almost always" for those who appear to be addicted. Nearly 46 percent of those who may be addicted report "feeling out of control" when they are online, and "almost always" logged on longer than they intended to. There is most probably a novelty effect for new Internet users, but the experience of losing track of time while online seems almost universal, and is much worse for those who are Internet addicted.

Many people initially report a compulsive-use pattern when they first go online, which typically decreases as the novelty wears off. However, there are clearly some people for whom this doesn't occur and who apparently ignore the warning signs of addiction. Although it's difficult to determine, it appears that you can get "stuck" in a pattern that continues to cause problems in your life. Many people only see themselves abusing the Net *after* it begins to interfere with their lives. Often this involves a spouse or family member expressing anger or concern that may begin to get their attention.

Open Twenty-Four-Seven—Accessibility

People love *accessibility*. They like being able to get what they want at any time. One of the chief attractions to the Internet is the incredible availability of the world's information—twenty-four hours a day, seven days a week. It's plugging into humankind's knowledge base at the touch of a button, all from the comfort of your living room! The Internet becomes a virtual supermarket of information with an infinite and varying selection. One self-confessed Nethead felt that the Internet was like a passport for the less affluent—being able to travel around the world, without ever leaving your home! He viewed the Net as a solid equalizer between economic classes.

The ability to instantaneously access a wealth of information can be highly arousing. This ease of accessing information creates a sense of power and accomplishment that hasn't previously existed in modern civilization's embrace of technology; this is technology everybody can use and get to function. It's the electronic convenience store of the information age and it's the place you go when you're hungry for information! In spite of delays, breakdowns, and constant glitches, people wait patiently to get their daily information fix. Many people I've interviewed report an almost irresistible urge to log on or check e-mail. If unable to do so for even one day, they report a noticeable withdrawal or discomfort.

Bigger Than Ourselves—Intensity

The Internet creates a sense of power, exhilaration, and *intensity*. People often express exhilaration and excitement with their ability to link onto larger systems at the push of a button. With a few keystrokes, they're able to tap into university databases, travel the world, visit the Library of Congress, have sex, improve their finances, look up medical information, and enjoy news, sports, and entertainment. However, all of this online research is done in a socially isolated and solitary manner, devoid of real-time human contact. It's interesting that online and cyber-relationships often seem to end up with real-time contact. There seems to be a natural need for real-time human connection, which is only simulated by the Internet, and not completely duplicated.

When we're alone with our computer too long some of us begin to have an *affair with it*, attempting to meet our emotional needs through cyberliving. About 20 percent of general Internet users make contact with and/or meet someone they are conversing with online, but among Internet addicts that figure jumps to nearly 50 percent! Thirty-one percent of Internet addicts have had a real-time sexual relationship with someone they met online. The personal connection you can have with your computer can produce an intense, and strong interpersonal, experience. This isn't TV. You can't really interact with your TV, and it's that social–technical interaction that produces the intensity. This is TV on steroids!

Time Has No Bounds—Timelessness

Time distortion is perhaps the most universally agreed upon online experience, with Internet addicts nearly always experiencing it, and most Internet users experiencing it sometimes. This experience of *timelessness* is described similarly to the passage of time during a casino gambling experience.

There are no markers of time while online. Almost everyone that goes online says that they lose track of time, and that surfing the net is often characterized by a sense of "being beyond time and space." Many people report that hours will go by, with little or no awareness of their surroundings or other commitments. This is one of the most significant indicators of the power of the Net. Experiences that can prompt you to forget who and where you are and create an altered state of consciousness are quite powerful. This isn't necessarily negative. Going to a good movie might produce the same result. However, a movie is temporary, and a true Nethead can't just surf for an hour. They get stuck, and they keep coming back. Just like a drug (without the hangover and illegality) the Internet has the power to change your emotional interface with the world!

The phenomenon of timelessness is known in psychological science as *dissociation*. It's a normal psychological mechanism commonly experienced when engaging in a stimulating, painful, and/or potentially addictive behavior. This is not unlike the experience of the casino gambler, who describes twelve hours passing by with little or no awareness, even forgetting to eat or go to the bathroom!

The casino is designed from its inception to enhance the experience of dissociation. The greater the sense of timelessness, the more time and money spent. For instance, clocks and windows aren't typically available as they provide cues for the time of day. There is little or no information about the outside world available to you when you're gambling. You're in a box. You are there to be focused, and the casino wants that focus to be on gambling. This is why they bring you drinks, and will provide your food and hotel; they want you as nearby as possible. (Is this beginning to sound familiar?) All of this is done to ensure that the gambler continues to gamble for as long as possible.

This is remarkably similar to many people's description of an Internet experience, with the endless *links* and *banners* to "click" onto, enticing you to stay just a little bit longer. *Links* and *banners* are virtual billboards that advertise another Website. You simply click on the link or banner and away you go. Links and banners are becoming a form of advertising and companies will place their banners on high-traffic sites as a means to reach potential customers. Each click provides a new psychological "hit" just as each roll of the dice promises the possibility of a win!

As in gambling, there are very few indicators of time passing while online. While intently staring at a video screen, you have very little awareness of the outside world. Your vision and focus become narrowed. You become part of your own world, a world in which you have the illusion of complete control and mastery. The outside world shrinks, receding into the background, and there is nothing except you and your computer. What could be more captivating and what could be more habit forming?

What's in a Name?—Anonymity

The Internet is the *ultimate* form of anonymity. Communicating on the Internet, especially in chat rooms, private rooms, MUDDING (Multiple User Digital Domain), and on sexual Web sites, allows a complete sense of *anonymity* and fantasy. Nobody knows who you really are, and *you can be anybody you want*.

There are some estimates that between 33–50 percent of individuals on the Internet are lying about some aspect who and what they are. Some people have even been found to represent themselves as members of the opposite sex! There is undoubtedly a considerable amount of lying about marital and financial status along with portraying one's personal characteristics as being more desirable than in reality. Everyone online weighs less than the real-time scale indicates! People become actors and actresses allowing their innermost fantasies to become expressed to others online.

All of this information sharing is done with little identifying information. And what is available, is difficult to verify. Other than the Internet, there are very few places in this world that allow you to create such a separate identity and live a virtually different life. This anonymity is the Internet's power, fun, and its curse, and it will probably change as accountability standards are developed by regulatory bodies. Just as caller ID has changed the way we use the telephone, the Web will eventually have easier means to identify its users.

The anonymity of the Net can also be positive, as in the case of online support groups, where identification would be considered less desirable. However, the Net's privacy has also contributed to the popularity of many potentially negative Web sites, including gambling, adult, and shopping sites. There are darker sides to anonymity, such as in the case of protecting even illegal or antisocial acts like making bombs or advocating hate crimes.

Let it All Hang Out—Disinhibition

Another phenomenon that's unique to the experience of the Internet is *disinhibition*. Disinhibition is the ability to express yourself in ways that you're not normally able to do. Due to the accessibility and anonymity that's experienced on the Internet, 80 percent of Internet addicts experience disinhibition, along with nearly 45 percent of all Internet users who feel uninhibited when online. People report this enhanced sense of freedom because the normal self-control and filtering that occur in the real-time world is absent. It's replaced by an exciting openness to express yourself in completely new ways.

Similar to acting, you can reveal aspects of your life that you might not ordinarily share, even with your spouse (or especially with your spouse). It can be like having a virtual support group—a safe place to express your innermost thoughts and feelings, where everyone reveals things about themselves without feeling judged or accountable. Disinhibition is also experienced as fun and exciting, which makes the Internet a place to look for new relationships as well as information.

Love at Light Speed—Accelerated Intimacy

Over 40 percent of Internet users experience what I call *accelerated intimacy*. You feel an increased sense of intimacy and social connection at a much faster than normal rate. Among Net addicts, accelerated intimacy jumps to 75 percent with little distinction between men and women. Because people communicate on the Net through typewritten messages, they'll reveal aspects of themselves to others in a more open and forthright manner. There appears to be a greater trust and perceived honesty with written communication as compared to other communication forms. When combined with anonymity and disinhibition, this can produce an intense sense of intimacy. Written communication can evoke greater intimacy (look at love letters), because it's encoded in our brains through multiple input channels. You *see* it, you *hear* the words as you read them to yourself, and you can interact and *touch* the text in three dimensions. You can also respond using the same modalities, which seems to produce a deeper input to the brain.

The word *intimacy* should be used with some caution, however, because it may also reflect *pseudo-intimacy*. The jury is still out on whether cyber-relationships will stand the test of time any better than their real-time equivalents, and whether real-time relationships that began on the Net have a different outcome than typical ways of relating. The disinhibition that people initially experience does foster a sense of *instant intimacy*, but this may or may not translate into a more mature, ongoing love.

I have seen numerous couples for marriage counseling following an extramarital affair that started online. In fact, a prominent family attorney recently noted to me that he has seen many couples recently whose divorce preceding were initiated because of an online affair. Some of these people left fifteen-year marriages because they felt closer to their cyber-friend than to their own spouse! They probably *were* closer in some ways, which speaks to the Net's allure, although it remains to be seen whether relationships spawned online will stand the test of real-time.

This heightened intimacy, coupled with the immediate gratification that's found from instantaneous communication, seems to produce the experience of intense and *accelerated intimacy*. Exactly why is this? It's probably in part because you can communicate on a more time-intensive (compressed) basis with cyberfriends than with your own spouse or partner, and a maxim for good real-time relationships is spending quality time together. If you use leftover time (that is, time that is left *after* you've done everything else) for your relationship, then you'll have a *leftover relationship!* Those individuals who are spending six, eight, or ten hours a day on the Internet cannot possibly have a significant contribution of quality time available to their spouse or other loved ones. Hence, time is often used in a more intensive manner when communicating to individuals on the Net, which further adds to the experience of powerful intimacy. If you spent that kind of time with a spouse or real-time friend, you could also experience greater intimacy, but it wouldn't have the relative ease of the Internet.

It may also be easier to experience romantic intimacy when the practical reality and anxiety of sexual consummation is not immediately present. Perhaps by removing the immediate possibility of sexual relations a delay is created whereby one is forced (or free) to develop greater depths of nonphysical communication. The Internet is perfect for this form of intimacy because the act of writing forces the use of alternate (and perhaps deeper) forms of communication. This may be the electronic equivalent of romantic love letters that have captured many a heart.

Just a Phone Call Away—Ease of Access

The Internet is readily available. Estimates are that there are several hundred million people currently online around the world, and that number is growing by as much as ten thousand per week in the United States alone. These numbers are so large, and change so fast, that it's nearly impossible to offer any clear prediction of the future.

One thing that is certain, however, is that as computer quality improves (including better sound quality, faster video images, and easier transmission of multimedia), the accessibility and attractiveness of the Internet will become greater. This, combined with faster modems, accessible Internet service providers, and lower costs for accessing the Internet, increases the practical availability of the Internet. And now that good computers are dropping to well below one thousand dollars, the Internet is taking its place next to the VCR and CD player as standard home entertainment appliances, with many homes having multiple computers and home-based networks.

Where else can you, at the push of a button, and with relative low cost, access virtually all information in the world?

Some of this information, such as sexually explicit material, is not easily available in other places. There are obviously many people who, because of the Internet, would not otherwise access such information. This also applies to other forms of information, including some that are being created or modified just for the Internet. The Net will continue to grow exponentially as *ease of access* jumps to the next level with super-fast modems and TV/computer integration. Web TV is a first step toward this change.

A Story That Never Ends—the Unending Process

I met John while taping a TV show on Internet addiction where he described himself as a true cyberholic. He'd use computers everywhere: at the library, friends' homes, banks, and schools—anywhere he could borrow a keyboard. This self-confessed Nethead recounted the phenomenon to which he attributes his intense Internet use. He felt a "sense of endless of opportunity" while online; online you're never *done* with your task as you might be when reading a newspaper or book. As long as there's always another *link* or *hypertext* to click on, or another site to visit, it's possible for you to never really experience a sense of completion.

This sense of an unending process while using the Internet, can be very stimulating. This sensation contributes to what is known in psychology as *the principle of incomplete Gestalts*. That is, we tend to remember and recount those events that are incomplete and unfinished. There's a natural desire for the mind to attend to those incomplete tasks. The subconscious mind, in its attempt to fully process and master information, will psychologically revisit the situation until it is complete.

Surfing the Net may actually derail this *natural closure* process with its endless boundaries and unending opportunity to show and tell. This is a compulsive's nightmare. You can *never* do enough, and even if you do, it can all change the next day! You never experience a sense of competence, because it's impossible to master something that is unending, which is in part why you keep going back for more—to master the situation.

Becoming Involved with Your Computer—Interactivity

The *interactive nature* of the Internet creates strong appeal to keep logging on. It is an attractive and easy way to immediately alter your reality. "Hot as Fire," for example, felt she was affecting her world in a new and powerful way, which she found very exciting. This was perhaps the most potent social interaction she'd *ever* experienced, and unlike TV, the Net offers a user the opportunity to be *part of the story!* You're both the participant and the observer, creating a dynamic and reciprocal process where all Net users virtually interact with each other. A digital dance of sorts, this interactivity gives the user an analog to social interaction and hence *some* of its attractiveness.

Many of the Internet's staunchest defenders even extol the Internet's ability to provide the next best thing to social interaction. The Net may then be seen as the modern day Main Street, with the added convenience and safety of never having to leave your home. This experience is both liberating and limiting, for in order to be logged on to the Web, you have to be *logged-off everywhere else* in your life, which can become a potential problem. Hence the reason for this book!

Where else can you achieve stimulating social and intellectual interaction with little physical and psychological effort? It's the American dream—social fast food. It's the next best thing to drive-through relationships. Anyone with a computer can safely and effortlessly alter his or her world quickly and anonymously. You can put your password in and download friendship. To many Netheads, the relationships they develop on the Web are very significant and real, even if they've never met the person they're talking to. The ease of cyber-relating becomes so attractive that it can easily become habitual. If you have any doubts, find out how many of your friends don't have the convenience of a dishwasher or microwave oven. Not too many, I would bet! We like convenience, and the Internet fits the bill.

Is it all bad? No. The Net can and does provide wonderful interpersonal connections, and it can fill a void in someone's life that perhaps would never otherwise be filled. The Internet is indeed a powerful tool that can be used, as well as abused. The key is recognizing when use becomes abuse, and when abuse becomes addiction!

Gambling and Surfing the Net—the Hypnotic Trance

There is some preliminary evidence that shows that staring at a monitor can induce a form of hypnotic trance. This can occur to some extent while watching TV as well, although I believe the hypnotic effect is heightened when sitting very close, as you would with a computer monitor. You might also increase your attention and concentration to the monitor because your visual field is so narrowed. There is theoretical evidence suggesting that the horizontal scanning lines (which move back and forth so fast that they're imperceptible) on a CRT (cathode ray tube) monitor are hypnotic inducing. You may be entering a trance-like state while online, which may be another reason why so many people seem to lose track of time while on the Net.

Of all the addictions that I've noted, the most similar multimedia stimulation to the Internet is gambling. To some extent, the parallels seem uncanny. When entering a casino, you have a variety of visually stimulating sites and locations to enter, not unlike the Internet. There is an influx of images, sounds, colors, and textures. Each gambling area is characterized by a unique experience, not unlike the different Web pages and Internet sites that one would log onto. Web surfing is like a night in the casino.

When you log on to a specific site or try to find a piece of information, there is a hit or miss (win or lose) quality to your search. A hit would be a completed connection, a stimulating site, or perhaps a cybersexual encounter. A miss would be a failed connection, the wrong URL, or a dead search. To some extent, you never know what you're going to find or experience when you log on, just as you never know whether you win or lose, which is part of the excitement. It's an adventure, one that takes over your time and money.

Preliminary research suggests a similarity between gambling and the Internet. Dr. Kimberly Young conducted a study of heavy Internet users, which found behavior patterns similar to compulsive gambling among Internet addicts. It seems that the stimulating effect of gambling parallels what Internet abusers typically report. They both report the excitement of not knowing what you're going to experience when you log on (or when you gamble) and that's part of the fun!

It's likely that nearly every individual in the United States knows someone, or has access to someone, who has access to the Internet. It's also likely that most people know someone who they think might be spending too much time online. Bill Gates, founder and CEO of Microsoft Corporation, Steve Case, founder and CEO of America Online (AOL), and other techno-wizards are betting on our thirst for Internet technology. The challenge will be to not let this technology rule our lives, but rather to have it serve us. It seems that moderation will perhaps now have to be practiced in front of the computer as well as the refrigerator door!

Multimedia Appeal

The new combinations of stereo sound, enhanced video, brilliant colors, and faster modem speeds make the Internet the closest thing to a legal psychedelic experience. It's highly attractive with all its flash and splash. Advertisers and Internet Service Providers know this, and will undoubtedly use all the same tools that are used on TV to market you. Already AmericaOnline looks a lot like a commercial TV station or magazine, and is collecting some hefty advertising fees. This advanced digital network, which is accessed by remote control, will enable us to never leave our homes, which is clearly a blessing and a curse. With its multimedia interactivity, the Internet is likely to make TV pale in its relative attractiveness as the Net becomes fully integrated into our living room entertainment systems.

3

Performing a Self-Diagnosis

Are You Getting High on the Net?

*The first step in a journey begins when you
determine that you need to go on one.*

The fact that substances, such as alcohol and other mood-
altering drugs, can create a physical and/or psychological
dependence is well known and accepted. Not simply an interest, but rather a *driven pattern of use* that can produce a negative impact on your life.

More recently, however, there has been an acknowledgement that the compulsive performance of certain *behaviors* may mimic the addictive process found with drugs, alcohol, and other substances. The addition of behaviors, such as gambling, food, sex, work, TV, exercise, and shopping, to the definitions of addiction and compulsion represents a big change in the psychology and addictionology fields. Previously it was believed that a substance was necessary to evoke the symptoms of tolerance and withdrawal. We now know this is not true. I've seen many people in my practice who are addicted to a variety of behaviors. And some of these people are reporting serious consequences to excessive Internet use.

Mike's story is fairly typical of the many stories that are reported to me. Mike is a fifteen-year-old high school student. He is a typical kid from a multimedia savvy generation. He found my Web site under Internet addiction and took my research survey. Mike e-mailed me asking if I had any suggestions for him as he thought he might have a problem. He was spending numerous hours online daily and it was beginning to affect his schoolwork. He was starting to feel that he had a problem with his Internet use and didn't know how to deal with it. When I asked him if he had seen a psychologist or therapist about this, he indicated that his psychologist didn't know about the Internet and was completely unfamiliar with the concept of compulsive Internet use. This is not an unusual situation, as most mental health professionals know little about Internet addiction.

Although Internet addiction isn't an epidemic by any means, Mike's case is not unique. Cases like his are most probably under-reported and under-recognized by mental health and addictions professionals. Many professionals in the medical or psychological community are only now starting to recognize numerous cases in their own practice that appear to involve problems with the Internet.

Is the Internet Your Repeated Pleasure?

Whether or not we label this new phenomenon as a *compulsion* or as an *addiction* is of little relevance to those whose lives are being negatively affected. Labels will not help you decide if you're engaging in any behavior compulsively. You must first ask yourself if you've ever felt compelled to do something, especially something that started off as *pleasurable, repeatedly*? Have you ever done so, even when you knew that the consequences might be negative? The answer for most of us is probably yes to both questions. The Internet can be your *repeated pleasure*, and it is a pleasure that you may seek to repeat, irrespective of any consequences.

Twenty years ago it was believed you couldn't become addicted to gambling. Now we accept compulsive gambling as fact. What gamblers always knew took the mental health community decades to accept and integrate into popular acceptance. It seems that any new application or idea is rarely accepted as truth until the idea is no longer new. For those who suffer with any addiction, this delay in professional acceptance can slow down treatment or intervention. The Internet is probably where gambling was twenty years ago, as we're only now becoming aware of the dark side of this exciting technology.

What happens when you do something regularly that is pleasurable? The answer is, you do it more, and the more you do it, the greater the likelihood that your behavior will become habitual. You might also be surprised to discover that there are neurochemical changes in the brain that occur during the addiction process which give you a "hit" just like a drug. If this "chemical high" were pleasurable enough, wouldn't this induce you to repeat this behavior? The answer is probably "yes" for certain people under the right circumstances. In order to answer this question specifically about the Internet, a broader definition of addiction is needed.

Defining Addiction

Do you find yourself spending virtually all your time alone with your computer? Has your life begun to become *unmanageable* because of your Internet use? Do you feel *powerless* to stop or cut down your use? If you can answer yes to these questions, you may meet the criteria for Internet abuse or addiction. Use the following questions to evaluate whether or not you may be experiencing a problem in your life:

- Does a substance or behavior elicit a clear change in your mood? And is that substance or behavior later sought and utilized to achieve its mood-altering effects?
- Does ingesting the substance or performing the behaviors interfere with your life in any way, shape, or form? That is, does it have a negative impact on your work, school, family, friends, relationships, etc.?

Not only are these definitions of addiction very practical, but they also serve as clues on how behavior may at times become addictive (often without our being aware of it). Sometimes it's easier for people who know you best to see changes in your behavior even before you do. This is true because we tend to adjust over time to the gradual changes in our lives.

Although there may be a problem (as recognized by others), it is not until *you* recognize how the problem is affecting you that recovery begins. If you can answer affirmatively to one or both of the previous questions, then you probably fit this practical definition of addiction. These are similar to the definitions used by the twelve-step, Alcoholics Anonymous program (AA). They may not seem very empirical, but they work in the everyday world. I credit AA's phenomenal success to these simple and practical definitions that most people can relate to. The chief components that are reflective of an addiction are feelings of powerlessness and unmanageability of one's life, and the negative effect this can produce.

Assessing Your Behavior

Let me give you an example. I perform a fair number of court-ordered alcohol and substance abuse evaluations. In many cases they have been pulled over for drunk driving (DWI/DUI), and as a condition of their arrest, they're to be evaluated in order to determine the need for treatment. Many of the people I evaluate have had two or three previous arrests for DWI/DUI, yet most of the time they're not aware that their behavior may reflect a problem in their life. Most often, they don't consider themselves to be alcoholics. More often than not, until I point out the fact that getting arrested may represent *an interference with their life,* they simply don't see it.

I recently saw a man who had two DWIs as well as a drug arrest, but could not see that *he had a problem with drugs or alcohol!* This is probably due to his not having felt negative effects of his behavior (even if it's obvious to others) while in the midst of an addictive cycle. Often it's the *consequences* and *problems* in life from addictive behavior that will lead us to examine our behavior patterns. No consequences often equals little motivation to change.

A Road to Recovery

Changing an addictive pattern always involves examining your behavior, motivations, insight, and judgments. However, when you begin a recovery process, the reasons why you became addicted to begin with aren't initially addressed. Instead, the main focus in the early stages of treatment is on *changing patterns of behavior* to begin the healing process. The remainder of this chapter will address general themes of addiction and help you determine whether you are addicted. Chapter 4 will offer more detailed methods for determining if you may have a problem with Internet abuse or addiction.

The term "addiction" is actually not used in the diagnostic manuals of psychology and psychiatry. Typically the terms *abuse, dependency, impulse problem,* and *compulsion* are used to describe most types of addiction. For the purposes of this book, the terminology is unimportant and I prefer more pragmatic methods of diagnosing addiction, which are as follows:

> *When you can't stop doing something that is bad for you, others notice it before you do.*

It is hard to see your own negative behavior. And addiction can include the development of *tolerance* and/or *withdrawal*, which can only be noticed from within. For practical purposes, addiction and abuse could be defined as follows:

> *Addiction involves a behavior or substance on which you are dependent and that is painfully difficult to stop. Abuse, on the other hand, may simply be a repeated pattern of use without tolerance or pain (withdrawal) as a result of trying to stop.*

What Can I Become Addicted To?

Again, the unfortunate truth is probably everything, or more specifically, *everything fun* and *pleasurable*. The Internet, just as gambling, is simply another stimulating form of pleasurable entertainment that can produce an addictive potential similar to drugs or alcohol. Remember, we are pleasure-seeking creatures, and pleasurable behaviors are almost always repeated (or we give it a good try at attempting to do so!). We're still animals, where the basic biological principle of increasing pleasure and minimizing pain is part of our daily behavior. If you ever doubt this just watch an infant or toddler trying to gain something they want and you'll see a less sophisticated version of yourself. We are in part motivated by this pleasure principle all the time, but we typically attempt to use adult compromises to counterbalance our innate hedonism.

This is not to say that we don't have other, more mature thoughts, feelings, and choices. Indeed we do have the ability to choose. However, while in an addiction cycle, our *ability to choose becomes significantly impaired*. This is the essence of addiction.

My Brain Made Me Do It

What all addictive behaviors have in common is the ability to impact neurochemical changes in brain chemistry. It is often these indirect neurochemical changes that make you feel so good. The chief neurotransmitters responsible for this brain "high" are most likely to be dopamine and norepinephrine. They produce a pleasurable sensation in the brain, which we experience as a "good feeling," which therefore increases the stimulating behavior. Just as in drug and alcohol use, these brain chemicals are, in part, responsible for improving our mood after exercise, sex, shopping, and Net surfing. The initial choice to use either a drug, alcohol, or the Internet is yours. However, once an addictive cycle begins, the choice is soon replaced by a less voluntary and more compulsive pattern of use.

The Addictive Paradox:
An Endless Cycle

Many behaviors can change your mood. They can make you feel better or worse, happy or sad, or change your view of reality. If you have any question about this, think about the last time you smelled a flower, exercised, listened to a piece of music, or fought with your spouse! Our behaviors change our emotions so frequently we tend to take it for granted. Many times we find these changes pleasant, and as I said before, pleasant things are likely to be repeated. Sometimes, however, these pleasurable behaviors become habitual, and if the stimuli for those "hits" are readily available, an *addiction,* or an *abuse,* is born.

Ending an addiction requires some discomfort and pain. Most of us don't like to feel any pain, we like pleasure. We'll typically tolerate pain only when we're assured of a likely payoff in the future. But what happens if we don't feel that we have any future? What if, because our life has become so unmanageable, it seems hopeless? Where then does the motivation come from? Herein lies the paradox of addiction. How do you break the endless cycle of discomfort, guilt, and shame that is relieved by continuing the addictive behavior, which causes more pain and discomfort? It is this cycle of behavior that continues to cause the greatest discomfort when trying to change an addictive pattern. Throughout this book you will find suggestions on how to break this cycle and end the addictive paradox.

Logging On—How Does It Start?

Suppose you've worked all week and you're tired and stressed. You just got paid and you find yourself bored, edgy, perhaps a bit lonely, and a little down in the dumps. Perhaps you didn't take enough time for yourself? Maybe, like many people, you ignored your deeper psychological needs while just trying to get through daily routines. Add some children to the equation, and it only becomes more difficult. You resign yourself to an evening of TV and high-fat ice cream, but those only hold you for a little while.

So you decide to head for your computer to see what's happening in cyberspace. Sound familiar yet? Suddenly, you find yourself more excited, and perhaps a bit more energetic. You notice a pleasant combination of arousal and anticipation. You find yourself in a chat room and see who's online. After an hour of surfing around, you get an IM (*instant message*) from someone who wishes to talk to you. You don't know this person, but they seem interested in you. You strike up a conversation and hit it off.

This pattern continues night after night. Soon you're scheduling more frequent rendezvous, and spending more and more time online. You may even schedule time with an online correspondent in an *electronic bedroom*, which is a private chat room where you can be virtually alone. Other cybernuts may likely join you as you begin to develop a virtual social life online.

Initially you may have felt a sense of euphoria, excitement, and exhilaration. For a short period of time, during and just after your Internet adventures, there was a sense of peace. People often report a sense of "endless boundaries" and "feeling connected to the whole world," which are pretty powerful feelings. This "high" is directly related to the changes in brain chemistry that we discussed previously, and sets the groundwork for the addictive cycle to begin. The actual addiction cycle starts when you begin to regularly seek this relief and pleasure on a consistent basis in order to regain that sense of excitement. This also acts to medicate the shame and guilt that comes from the negative consequences of your extended time online. Soon the high is replaced by a simple reduction of discomfort; a familiar habit that just keeps you on an even keel. This provides additional fuel for the addiction cycle to maintain itself. When this pattern is continued on a repeated basis you can develop an Internet addiction.

In my practice and research, I have seen people spend up to sixteen hours, or more, a day online. At times, I have seen them neglect their spouse, children, friends, family, jobs, and school. In the earlier days of the Internet (only a few short years ago), people would run up huge telephone and ISP (Internet Service Providers) bills in the thousands of dollars. The consequences might even require them to file bankruptcy or to make significant sacrifices in lifestyle. Perhaps even more devastating than the financial consequences are the disruptions to your marriage, family, or job. Often, it's the emotional impact and consequences on loved ones that are the most devastating. All addictive behavior patterns, including Internet and the computer, can create this addictive cycle.

These are typical occurrences dealt with in most mental health practices today. Often, however, the psychologist or therapist may not ask the right questions about addictions in your life, and this is especially so with regard to the Internet. In fact, if you go into many homes today there is a good likelihood that you may find some form of compulsive behavior or addiction. The type and degree will vary, but the basic themes are similar.

If It Gets You High, It's All the Same

Often people separate the consumption of substances, such as alcohol, drugs, or food, from compulsive behaviors, creating an artificial distinction between them. This is probably because of the drug's obvious and immediate chemical effects. What I'm proposing is that on a neurochemical level, the act of creating *any* pleasurable sensation *also* creates a chemical change in the brain. Whether that chemical sensation is caused by a behavior, such as gambling, sex, eating, shopping, or the Internet, or by the ingestion of a drug, is largely irrelevant. How you get to that *out-of-control place* doesn't really matter. The fact that you are there makes all the difference in the world. But it only makes a difference if you're conscious of *your addictive pattern!*

Why Me?

The reasons that some people develop a problem while others do not are not clearly understood. Addictions research suggests that addiction comes from a combination of factors, including heredity, family history, diet/nutrition, levels of stress, general health, psychological functioning, along with the potency of the source addiction. All of these factors combined contribute to the likelihood that an individual will find that they're addicted to a certain behavior or mood-altering drug.

There is no such thing as an "addictive personality." Addiction is a human problem or illness that affects many people (there are estimates that as many as twenty million people are affected in the United States by drugs and alcohol alone).

There are millions more living addicted lifestyles involving a variety of behaviors including, sex, gambling, Internet, food, shopping, and TV. It's yet another example of our imperfect humanity.

It is *not* a character weakness that determines your susceptibility to addiction. Many of the patients whom I've treated for addiction were successful, intelligent, and insightful people. They often report that the "one" (and sometimes only) problem they couldn't solve on their own was their addiction. And it took them some time to come to this conclusion. It didn't seem to matter what they were addicted to. The only thing that mattered was that they felt helpless in controlling it themselves, often with years of unsuccessful attempts at cutting back or discontinuing use!

4

Are You a Nethead?

The Warning Signs of Internet Abuse and Addiction

Anything that feels good can be addictive.

There are clearly many things that motivate people to become and remain addicted to destructive behaviors. However, there are many more unanswered questions with regard to Internet use and abuse. For instance, psychologists don't know exactly why some people become addicted while others do not, or what makes the Internet in particular so addictive. It is most likely a combination of the social aspects (chat, e-mail, private rooms) and the strong sexual elements of the Internet that become so habit forming. Other theories include the attractiveness of the multimedia stimulation, availability of knowledge, and so on.

Whatever the particular reasons are, if you're abusing the Net, it's time to take action and get your life back on the right track. This chapter will review some typical warning signs of abuse and addiction, and provide a series of steps that you can take to reclaim your life from cyberspace. It's time to begin *real-time living.*

Real-Time Living

Real-time living is simply *living with less technology,* or using it less often. Real-time living is having your technology serve you instead of becoming a slave to it. After all, if you are compulsively using techno-tools like the Internet, how can you be fully free to enjoy your life? *Virtual Addiction* can help you begin to shift the scales of balance back to having free choice about how you spend your time and energy. Technology can only serve you when you apply self-discipline and resist the continual seduction that the Internet offers.

How to Understand Your Level of Abuse

First, review the warning signs of abuse and addiction in this chapter to determine if you have a problem and to what extent. The following chapters will then help you to deal with specific problem areas in your life, and offer more detailed strategies for overcoming Internet addiction.

Technology: The Modern Sword of Damocles

Technology is bound by no moral code. Any meaning it has comes from the humanity which imbues it. The Internet exists and progresses simply because we know it *can be done and how to do it*. The Internet is an example of a technology that has a mind of its own and is on a path of seemingly endless growth. Computers and the Internet are not evil, but they can sap your time and energy with little awareness on your part, so it's important to ask questions anytime that you embrace technology. We must continually take stock of the impact the Internet has on our lives, as science and technology will undoubtedly continue. All of this will do us little good, unless we continue to develop our understanding of the "human side of the machine."

Like many of you, I like technology. What's not to like? With its gadgets and gizmos, technology offers the promise of new and more efficient ways to do things. More efficiency and more productivity, but at a price. The price for a better tomorrow usually requires a seemingly endless immersion in techno-babble with little hope of mastery; you're always behind the technological eight ball, because you can't possibly keep up with the knowledge curve. One has the sense that if you don't have the latest processor, fastest modem, or the newest software upgrade you're somehow lacking. I call this phenomenon *processor envy*!

Many of my patients and friends view themselves as technologically impaired because they're caught between the old analog world and the promises of the digital wonderland. People often feel they'll miss something if they aren't on the high-tech bandwagon, and to some extent they're correct. The problem is that there's no way to truly master the quixotic nature of high technology. There's no better example of this than the Internet. How can you master a world that changes every day? One must develop an acceptance of the impossibility of the situation, in order not to be compelled to keep up with technology.

The Lure of the Ultimate Gadget

The computer is a technological wizard. It can do what is otherwise impossible, and it can do so quickly and efficiently. If the computer represents a hallmark of technology, the Internet represents the boundless application frontier. The Internet offers the promise of new and exciting opportunity as it bespeaks of all that we hold dear. Throw in a little multimedia stimulation and you've got entertainment (look out, TV), add in all the information on the planet, and you've got *edutainment.* (a combination of educational and entertaining information.). The certain integration of the Internet and TV will undoubtedly expand this attraction, for once the computer and the TV are melded (Intelavision) into a seamless system, it will truly bring the Internet to the masses. (Web TV is a start in this direction.) This will make the Internet as easy as clicking your remote. No mouse to coax, no need to log on, and no need to wait for downloads; this quicker and easier version of the Internet will appeal to just about everyone. The vision of the future Internet, which is discussed in more detail in chapter 12, will be an immediately accessible and ever-present connection into the information superhighway.

Research shows the average use among nonaddicted Net users seems to be around six hours a day! For those of you that are addicted to the Net (about 6 percent) you tend to spend a lot more time online, probably close to nine hours a day! There doesn't seem to be a big difference between men and women in their Internet use.

As the Internet became mainstream, psychologists began to see the early signs of the power of the Internet from reports by patients. I began to see couples where a spouse was having an affair online; employees entrenched on the Net while at work; or mothers who were spending so much time on the Net that they were neglecting their kids. There are also a growing number of men and women who are using the Internet as a high-tech meat market for love, sex, and romance. I was stunned to hear the number of patients in our practice (and from e-mails I received) that used the Net to find sexual partners, often meeting with them at their homes after a brief cyberaffair.

Dangers of the Techno-Lure

In assessing the usefulness of any new technology, it is important to always balance its value with your quality of life and overall health. Work, friends, family, hobbies, and your physical, spiritual, and emotional health are areas of your life that cannot be formatted, compressed, and digitized. They reflect the *qualitative* flavor of life that gives meaning to our existence. Fortunately, most of what is really good in life cannot be reduced to bits of data. The Internet, however, does seem to possess a unique combination of both *interpersonal* and *technical* attractiveness, thereby attracting a wide audience of users and at times confusing our focus on what is truly important.

Rebecca's story is not unusual of someone whose Internet use became addictive. She explained to me in a therapy session that she was spending twenty to thirty hours a week looking for men to meet online. One week that she described as quite successful, she managed to meet two men, one of whom traveled from a neighboring state to spend the weekend with her. She spent the weekend having sex with this man she only knew for a few hours. Another week there was a guy who flew in from across the country for a week of real-time sexual adventure. Although exciting, these encounters often left her feeling used and empty.

Rebecca, like many other men and women who use the Internet addictively, are finding that their online behavior is not the only thing that is out of control in their life. Rebecca lead a busy life. She often had too much to do and allowed little time to socialize. She was lonely and perhaps a bit shy and socially awkward.

The preliminary results from our research support previous findings where heavy Internet users (those spending six to nine hours a day or more) demonstrate similar behavior patterns to gambling addicts. I have identified *seven critical signs* that seem to predict the likelihood that you are Internet addicted. They are as follows:

The Seven Critical Signs of Internet Addiction

1. You spend many hours online, often neglecting or in place of, other crucial areas in your life (the more hours spent online the more likely you'll be addicted).

2. Your friends and loved ones think you have a problem with your Internet use (the more people who think you have a problem, the greater the chance that you're addicted).

3. Your age matters—the younger you are the greater the likelihood you'll be addicted (you are more likely to be addicted if you're in your twenties).

4. You've had serious negative consequences from your Internet use.

5. You perceive your Internet experience as intensely intimate.

6. You keep the amount of time you spend online a secret.

7. You can't wait to get on the computer or Internet on a regular, even daily, basis.

If all seven criteria are true of you, there's a very high likelihood that you are Internet addicted or at least seriously abusing the Internet.

The Twelve Warning Signs and the Internet Abuse Test

If you or a family member are worried that you may be too involved with the Internet, then taking this simple self-test may help you determine if you have a problem with your Internet use. Here are twelve warning signs that may indicate that you are getting lost in cyberspace. If you can answer yes to between *three* and *five*, then consider taking a look at the time and energy you spend online.

You might consider examining your Internet use pattern and attempt to cut down. If you answer positively to *six* or more, then you may have a more serious problem and should take the eleven-question Virtual Addiction Test (VAT) found toward the end of the chapter.

Take Note

The following criteria should in no way serve as a diagnosis, but rather as general guidelines toward identifying a problem, as currently there are *no formal* or scientifically validated criteria for Internet abuse, dependency, or addiction. There is some current research on Internet addiction, but few studies to date have empirically proven what most Internet researchers suspect—that the use of computers, and especially the Internet, can produce a compulsive behavior pattern with potential serious implications.

If you answer positively on the Internet Abuse Test (IAT) or the Virtual Addiction Test (VAT), then you may very well have a problem with Internet addiction and should consider consulting a psychologist or other mental health professional with expertise in addiction. Be sure it is someone familiar with compulsive/addictive behavior patterns such gambling, sex, or eating, as these doctors are likely to be more accepting of the possibility of being addicted to the Internet. Remember this is a fairly new problem, and it not yet widely understood by mental health experts. The tests and questionnaires simply serve as warning signs and guidelines for informational and educational purposes only. They are not a substitute for professional treatment services, although they can assist you in beginning your own process of recovery and change.

Internet Abuse Test (IAT)

1. You spend an excessive amount of time in online chat rooms, particularly in the rooms having to do with sex or sexuality, or in private rooms engaged in sexual conversations and/or cybersex.

2. You find yourself gravitating toward one or more individuals with whom you have regularly scheduled, or unscheduled, but desired contacts.

3. You find yourself becoming depressed or lonely as you spend more time online.

4. You have made numerous attempts to have other contact with individuals on the Net, either by phone, in writing, or meeting in person.

5. You find yourself hiding information from your spouse, significant other, friends, or family regarding the amount of time and/or your activities on the Internet. In other words, you find yourself being secretive about the nature and the extent of your use.

6. You were initially excited when you came upon a stimulating situation accidentally on the Internet, but now actively seek it out each time you log on to the Net.

7. You constantly have thoughts about using the Internet for purposes of making sexual connections and/or fulfilling your social and interpersonal needs

8. You find the anonymity of online interactions to be more stimulating and satisfying than your real-time relationships.

9. You find it difficult to stop logging on to the Internet and feel compelled to do so on a daily basis.

10. You experience guilt or shame about your use of the Internet.

11. You engage in active fantasy or masturbation while online, perhaps to the exclusion of sex with your partner or spouse.

12. You find that significant individuals in your life, including your significant other, spouse, friends, or family, are becoming troubled with the amount of time and/or energy you're devoting to the Internet. For example, someone significant in your life is complaining about your absence due to the excessive amount of time you're spending on the Net.

Your IAT score: _____

3–5 = warning; 6+ = probable Internet abuse problem

Sometimes there are more serious results of your compulsive use of the Internet. This occurs when excessive use or abuse escalates into an addiction. The addiction criteria that follow address a more advanced state of compulsive Internet use. The following tentative criteria for Internet addiction roughly parallel the psychiatric diagnosis for compulsive or pathological gambling, as it seems there is a similarity between the two problems.

It's not only the *amount* of time spent online that determines compulsive Internet use, but rather the *combination* of various negative behaviors that can produce significant problems in your life.

Virtual Addiction Test (VAT)

If you believe you have a more serious problem, and you have *six or more* warning signs of Internet abuse as measured by the Internet Abuse Test (IAT), you should take the Virtual Addiction Test (VAT) below. If you answer yes to *five or more* of the questions on *this* test than you may have an Internet addiction problem.

1. Do you feel "out of control" when using the Internet; e.g., feel "carried away"?

2. When not on the Internet, do you find that you're preoccupied with the Internet or computers (e.g., thinking about or reliving past experiences on the Internet, planning your next experience on the Internet, or thinking of ways to gain access to the Internet in the future)?

3. Do you find that you need to spend greater amounts of time on the Internet to achieve satisfaction similar to previous events?

4. Do you find yourself seeking more sexually stimulating material in order to achieve the same result as previously? (Tolerance symptoms.)

5. Have you repeated unsuccessful efforts to control, cut back, or stop using the Internet?

6. Do you feel restless or irritable when attempting to cut down or stop using the Internet? (Withdrawl symptoms.)

7. Are you using the Internet as a way of escaping from problems or relieving a bad mood (e.g., feelings of helplessness, guilt, anxiety, or depression)?

8. After spending what you consider an excessive amount of time on the Internet and vowing not to do so the next day, do you find yourself back on the next day or soon after?

9. Do you find yourself lying to family members, therapists, or others to conceal the extent of your involvement with the Internet?

10. Do you find yourself committing illegal acts related to your use of the Internet?

11. Have you jeopardized or lost a significant relationship, educational, or career opportunity because of your Internet use?

Your VAT score: _____

If you score *five* or more, there is a reasonable probability that you are addicted to the Internet.

If you answered positively to the Internet Abuse Test warning signs or the Virtual Addiction Test, it may be helpful to again ask yourself the following two questions that were initially presented in chapter 2. If either of your self-tests indicate that you have a problem, follow the suggestions offered in chapters 5–9.

- Does your Internet use elicit a clear change in mood? And is your continued Internet use later sought out and utilized to achieve its mood-altering effects?

- Does using the Internet interfere with your life in any way, shape, or form? That is, does it have a negative impact on your work, school, family, friends, relationships, etc.?

Both of these questions are very important. The second question is perhaps more relevant with regard to clarifying your addiction potential. We all do things we like or find exciting because of the way it makes us feel; it's assumed that most individuals who use the Internet find it pleasurable. On an intellectual basis, it satisfies many needs, including curiosity, knowledge, convenience, access to data that is not ordinarily available, and connecting with people on a personal or sexual basis.

However, when you use the Internet as a means to gratify what might otherwise not feel fulfilling to you, then your pleasure from online life may be superseding your satisfaction with real-time living. When this occurs there may be a potential problem, for although computers and the Internet aren't in and of themselves dangerous, the preference for cyberlife over real-time life should be viewed with some trepidation. The essence of an addiction then, is a repetitive pattern of Internet behavior which, in spite of certain negative consequences, is still continued.

When a problem behavior affects daily living, then we begin to look at how it fits into your life. If the Internet is interfering with your life, this is a good litmus test for determining whether you have a problem with Internet addiction. Remember, the definition of a problem is *a solution that no longer works*. The Internet may start out as fun (and for many people it stays that way) but for about 6 percent of you, it can cause real and lasting problems.

Although no formal psychiatric diagnosis of Internet addiction currently exists, there appears to be sufficient clinical and research evidence to support that an addictive phenomenon occurs when certain people utilize the Internet. It should be noted that many people, when they first get online, feel they're becoming addicted to the Net. This is fairly typical, and probably reflects a "novelty factor" that usually wears off in a short period of time. Many people report spending ten hours a day online at first, but this often decreases as one becomes accustomed to the experience.

5

Taming Your Cybertooth Tiger

What to Do if You Think You Are a Nethead

The future is the present done differently.

This chapter will offer general guidelines for dealing with Internet abuse and addiction. First I will present some methods for identifying whether or not you have a problem, followed by more specific techniques that can help you to reduce your compulsive Internet use. Many of these techniques have been used for years in the treatment of other addictions, and have a good track record. Some of the suggestions are new and are uniquely applicable to the Internet. While this chapter offers general steps you can take to end an addiction, the more specific Internet issues and solutions are discussed in chapters 6 through 10.

The First Step

What do you do if you think you're an Internet addict? First (and perhaps most importantly) you need to acknowledge the fact that the Internet may be problem for you and that your use of the Internet has interfered with your life in some way. This is the first key to your recovery process.

Sex, Lies, and the Internet

If your use of the Internet has become abusive, you're probably aware of the particular areas in your life that have suffered. Your problem may be that you're having an online affair, that your spouse is irritated with your spending too much time online, or that your work performance is deteriorating due to how much time you spend online at work.

In some cases, the effects are far more serious. A patient of mine claimed that her husband became addicted to the Net and met someone online. She felt that the Internet was definitely responsible for ending her marriage. Stories like this are becoming more frequent than you might think!

The list of potential consequences for Internet abuse is endless. People have been fired for downloading pornography or other adult information at work. I recently heard about an adult Web site that changed the name of their chat room to sound more innocuous, so as not to draw attention from employers! In another instance an attorney consulted with me because he was representing someone who'd been arrested for viewing child pornography online. Recently, I was even contacted about two cases where suspected child neglect was being investigated due to heavy Internet use by one of the parents. Fortunately, you're reading this book. And hopefully you're willing to make some changes and learn how to strike a balance with your Internet use.

Define Your Problem

Do you find yourself lying about your Internet use to your friends or family? Are you spending more time than you'd like to when you go online? Is your Internet use starting to interfere with your life? Are other people expressing concern to you about your Internet use? Are you having trouble getting things done in your life because of the amount of time you spend online? These questions (and others) may be helpful in defining your problem with the Internet.

When a person comes into my office and states that he or she may be addicted to something, whether it be drugs, alcohol, or the Internet, the first thing that I do is assess how their behavior has had a negative impact on the quality of their lives. It's presumed at this time that the person has admitted to themselves and others that they in fact *do* have a problem. Every individual has a different degree of tolerance for the negative effects that addictive or abusive behavior may cause in their lives. Usually, however, every person has their *bottom line*, at which point they will recognize that their life has become *unmanageable*. Unfortunately, sometimes a serious loss may have to occur prior to such recognition.

First assess what has become *unmanageable* in your life. You can do this by reviewing the major areas of your life and determining whether or not the time you spend in cyberspace has had a negative impact on your work, schooling, marriage or relationship, health, or finances. Remember that any time you spend online is time *not spent* on other parts of your life! Many times the Net-effect is on a marriage due to cyberflirting or cyberaffairs, which are discussed further in chapters 6 and 7. The bottom line is that until you've clearly seen your Internet use impact your life in a negative way, you *may not* recognize it as a problem. Many people have e-mailed me stating that they love the Internet and it's not a problem for them, that they simply choose to use it a lot. I agree with this statement. Internet use is not a problem unless and until it stops you from enjoying some other aspect of your life. Frequently, however, the addictive process blinds you from seeing the true affect on your life.

You may have to also ask yourself whether anyone else sees your online behavior as a problem. One of the best predictors of Internet addiction is when someone notices your excessive-use pattern enough to mention it to you. I have seen several patients and received e-mail from angry husbands and wives about their spouse's Internet use. Interestingly, this seems to occur equally for men and women!

Because time can pass easily while online, it often takes people several months, or even longer, before recognizing a problem with their Internet use. Almost all Netheads report losing track of time and spending longer stretches online than they'd intended. After all, you're having fun. It's precisely because of the fun of being online that the detrimental effects of the Internet can elude you.

One word of caution deserves note here—don't dismiss computers and the Internet as the problem. This is far from the truth, as it would be an overly simplistic conclusion. Rather, *any behavior,* including the Internet, practiced to the exclusion of other important aspects of your life, can hamper the quality of your living, leading to negative consequences. The Internet has such a potential. The key is to learn to have Internet technology serve you, while not becoming a slave or a victim of its power.

Many people who are addicted or abusing the Internet e-mailed me about how the Internet has had a positive impact on their lives. For some of you, it may be a way to overcome your social fears, shyness, or physical limitations. These can all be limiting factors to real-time relating. There are also those of you who just enjoy the Internet and view it as an alternative form of communication and entertainment. None of these reasons are inherently bad. They become a problem when your time online creates a negative effect in some way. I would further add that if you're not developing your potential elsewhere, then you're probably limiting yourself. While the Internet is great for a lot of things, it isn't a long-term substitute for living a full life in my opinion. Cyberliving is fun and exciting, but I believe there can be a narrowness in the lives of those who live theirs in a virtual reality.

Abuse Versus Addiction

Many people I talk with about Internet addiction do not fit the definition of an addict. They do however fit the definition of an *Internet abuser*. The main difference being that the abuser does *not* seem to suffer from *tolerance* or *withdrawal*, and tends not to experience as many *serious consequences* of their Internet use. If you're an Internet abuser, you can learn to change the way you use the Internet. You can take steps to alter your dysfunctional patterns of use.

The first way is to use the Net only when you *need to do a specific job*. This means use the Internet *only* as a tool to retrieve e-mail, check stocks, or buy an airline ticket, not as entertainment. Decide on the needed task *ahead of time,* log on, find what you want, and then *log off* quickly. Many people who use this method find that it enables them to get a job done using the Internet, and that they don't feel so carried away every time they use it. It does take some discipline, but it seems to work for a majority of Net abusers. Internet addicts may not be able to use this technique as it may retrigger their addiction; abstinence from the Internet may become necessary for these addicts, at least on an initial basis.

It's probable that the vast majority of Internet users who are having problems with the Net fall into an abuse, as opposed to an addiction, category. When you abuse something you tend to use it compulsively at times, but not consistently. Addiction reflects a difficulty in discontinuing without significant discomfort. A relatively small percentage (approximately 6 percent) of Internet users could be classified as addicted, but the actual numbers are huge due to the millions of people currently online. Even if you do not meet the full criteria for an addiction, you may just be spending too much time on the Net. And you might be deriving far too much personal gratification online, to the exclusion of other aspects of your life.

The Net Effect

Most of my patients don't initially express their primary concern being Internet use or addiction. Indeed, many times it's not even brought up in the context of my first interview with my patients. In the course of conducting clinical interviews, however, I've found that, though the presenting problem was marital stress, it's at times attributable to a husband or wife spending *excessive amounts of time* on the Internet. It is also often the case that they are spending excessive time on the Net *in response* to their marital problems.

No matter how you look it, if you're online, say, from six P.M. to two A.M. every night, you cannot be spending the necessary quality time to develop and maintain an emotional life with your spouse or family. This is bound to have implications for any marriage.

Another increasingly common reason that people come in for marriage counseling, is that a spouse has discovered that his or her partner is having an online affair, or *cybersex*. (In the next chapter, the nature of online affairs is discussed and the delicate balance between cyberflirting and having an affair is addressed.)

Abstinence or Controlled Use?

There is an age-old controversy in addiction treatment as to whether someone can stop an addiction while still doing the drug or the behavior on a modified basis. For certain drugs, including alcohol, it is widely believed that abstinence is essential to maintaining sobriety. For addictive behaviors such as sex, eating, work, gambling, or the Internet, the issue becomes more complex. Many of these behaviors cannot be avoided. We must eat to live, and sex is typically part of our lives, and the same goes for work. Other behaviors such as gambling and the Internet are *not* necessary to live, so one could theoretically abstain from them indefinitely. This may prove difficult and impractical for many people, however.

Whether or not you have to give up using the Internet permanently in order to deal with an Internet addiction problem will depend on your particular behavior pattern. Although we can safely say that one must be abstinent from gambling in order to maintain recovery, this may not be the case with the Internet. The best assumption at this point would probably be that it depends upon the degree and pattern of Internet abuse, along with one's personal circumstances in determining whether controlled use is possible.

My best plan for dealing with Internet abuse or addiction would at the very least include a significant reduction in use, and/or *limiting how, when,* and *why* you use the Net. Changing your pattern of use can go a long way in transforming a compulsive behavior to a more manageable one. For some people, however, abstinence will be necessary (at least for a while) in order to break the addictive cycle. After the addiction cycle is broken, you *may* be able to resume moderate use.

Some Basic Guidelines

The following are offered as basic guidelines to assist you in making the needed changes in your life that will help you address your Internet abuse or addiction. *Virtual reality* is often easier than real life. Cyberspace poses few of the complex interpersonal challenges that real-time living requires. Online, everything can be finished in a nanosecond or you can simply turn off your problems at any time. If you don't like someone you're talking to, you can log off. If you don't like the information you're viewing, you can reload. If you don't like the link you're on, you can simply find another one. Real life, however, is not this simple. Real life is messy.

Again, you must acknowledge the degree to which you find yourself unable to take control of your use of the Internet. This may be hard to do on your own. Sometimes a friend or family member can help you to see yourself more objectively. The first step to healing any problem is to acknowledge that there is a problem. This may be quite difficult for Internet addiction, insofar as it's not yet an openly recognized or discussed problem in our society. Although there are addiction support groups available for the Internet, many of them are located on the Internet. This may reduce their effectiveness for addicts and inadvertently lead to further social isolation.

The following are *thirteen general suggestions* to help you in dealing with Internet addiction or abuse.

Thirteen Ways to Reclaim Real-Time Living

These thirteen techniques are applicable to anyone who is either abusing or addicted to the Net. The suggestions can also help promote general health and well-being. These guidelines should serve as a starting point in making the desired changes to your Internet problem. There are further suggestions offered in chapters 6, 7, 8, and 9.

1. **Consider taking a technology holiday.** Turn off the computer. Don't use it on a daily basis. If you have to use it, use it only for necessary tasks. Force yourself to go off-line, and say good-bye temporarily (or possibly permanently) to those people you're conducting a life with on the Internet. You can start this in a gradual way by creating a computer / Internet-free day, gradually extending this to include larger periods of time.

   The reason for this is simple. You want to begin to train your nervous system to recognize that you can tolerate a day or an evening without something that you *need* to use on a consistent basis. Until you demonstrate to your mind and body that this can be done, you are going to continue the repetitious cycle of your behavior. The important thing to remember is that change has to start somewhere. If you make no change in your life, time will continue to pass anyway, and it will pass *just as easily* as you begin to make small changes in your life. *Dysfunctional behavior is simply the resistance to change.* This is actually the same as the insistence that something be different, in spite of making no efforts to change it!

For example, Steve had to use his computer and the Internet every day for work. His job involved online sales in the insurance industry. The problem was that he could not stop logging on to adult Web sites. It was beginning to interfere with his work, and he was getting complaints from his superiors. As a result, Steve decided to take some time away from the Net, and he changed the way he did his work. He would only go online when he absolutely had to, and began to depend more on the phone and fax. Within three weeks he was able to take more control of his Internet use and with the help of a therapist, he began to address his sexually compulsive behavior.

2. **Develop other interests.** Your new interests should have nothing to do with computers or the Internet. Try a new activity or hobby. Do something active, preferably with your body, as the Net is very cerebral. It would be even better if that hobby or activity could include your spouse, friend, or significant other, fulfilling some of your social needs previously met on the Internet. Force yourself to expand what you think you can do and try something new—it doesn't matter what. The idea is to expand your repertoire of interests and to provide new options for your entertainment and social needs.

   For example, the Net and computers weren't enough to satisfy John's craving for intimacy. He was spending hours a day corresponding with people in chat rooms. He initially found it very rewarding. But he soon found that his life was becoming too narrow, and almost boring. He was avoiding real-time friends, and was no longer going to the gym or reading. He even gave up his weekly basketball game in deference to his nightly Internet time. After a while he was doing nothing but sitting at his computer, like a chair potato, staring at the fifteen-inch monitor until he was blurry-eyed!

   After five sleepless nights, John decided to get a real life. He turned off the computer and set a goal of only one hour a day of time online. It worked! Within four weeks he was back to his old self, doing the activities he loved to do. He even enrolled in an art class at the local community college. Most importantly he was happier than he was when spending five hours a day on the Net talking to his cyberfriends.

3. **Exercise.** There is probably no one single recommendation that I can make that can have as many positive effects on your life as exercise. Exercise offers a variety of potential benefits. It's fun; can improve your health; boost your longevity; improve your overall functioning on a daily basis; control your weight; increase your energy; improve your mood; and improve your self-esteem.

There is research supporting the efficacy of exercise for improving psychological and addiction problems. There is also evidence in the literature that many addictive behaviors produce changes in the neurotransmitter *dopamine*. This is what may produce the "kick" or "high" for behaviors such as: gambling, compulsive eating, the Internet, alcohol, or drugs. Dopamine is responsible for a change in brain chemistry that feels good, and it is this "good feeling" that contributes to the repetition of the behavior. It seems plausible that Internet addicts may be experiencing these chemical changes when online, although how this occurs is not fully understood. Exercise may serve to replace some of the lost dopamine from decreasing Internet use, thereby allowing for an easier adjustment. Before starting *any* exercise program, you should consult your physician or other healthcare practitioner.

For example, Laurie was overweight. She often referred to herself as "fat." Laurie found a lot of comfort in eating (dopamine again!) and had always struggled with a weight problem. It was a losing battle for her. The Internet came at just the right time. She found many new friends online. She was delighted. Laurie even found a chat room devoted to heavy women and the men that love them. She spent hours online every day. Initially she felt great, but she noticed that she was beginning to gain more weight. She realized that she was eating a lot while she was online. She also realized that surfing the Net is *not* an aerobic sport, and she needed to become more active.

Eventually Laurie got on the scale after several months of compulsive Internet use. It read over two hundred pounds! She had gained over forty pounds in less than six months, and there were no signs of the weight gain slowing. What she saw that morning triggered something inside of her—for Laurie, this was *hitting bottom*. The next day she went out and hired a personal trainer and a nutritionist. She said good-bye to her chat room friends for a while, and began to cut her Net use down to a minimum. She replaced some of her cyberlife with time at the gym. She began to lose the weight, even to a point where she weighed less than she did prior to her Internet use. She also began to notice something else. She was beginning to feel better. Her mood was going up as her weight went down. She felt less depressed, and had a lot more energy. After a while Laurie didn't miss the time she spent online, although she still kept in touch with some of her cyberfriends.

4. **Watch less television.** I am convinced that the use and abuse of television exacerbates many problems in our society (especially violence). There appears to be a correlation between heavy TV use and Internet addiction for some people. Television is a passive activity that takes your time and energy and gives you little in return. Although there are many positives about television, it has a powerful capacity to waste your time just as the Internet can. Further, it can detract from the time you could use to focus on your relationships or other activities in your life. There are even some preliminary studies demonstrating a hypnotic effect from staring at the monitor (CRT screen) that may be caused by the rapid scanning of the video images. I recommend that you reduce the number of hours you watch TV or designate TV-free days. You would be amazed what you can do at home when you're not sitting and staring at the "tube"!

David and Leslie, for example, had been married only four years. They'd just had a baby when they came to see me for marriage counseling. Their marriage had really gone downhill after the baby was born (which is not all that unusual). It seems that David began retreating to watch TV after dinner every night, while Leslie was bathing and caring for their son. This problem seemed to come out of nowhere, but it did seem to start to get worse around the time they got their new computer with a cable modem. David seemed to toggle back and forth between the TV and the computer every night, spending almost six hours a day between both. Leslie would end up going to bed every night alone and she soon became angry and resentful. Any time that they managed to spend together was in front of their TV, with conversations being limited to commercial breaks. No marriage can thrive on sixty-second sound bites!

I suggested they consider reducing their TV viewing time and that David begin to limit his time at the computer. They began going to sleep at the same time and both reported an almost miraculous change in the way they felt about each other. They continued this plan after their counseling and still limit their TV and computer use. What's really interesting is that neither David nor Leslie feels they miss TV or the computer.

5. **Talk to your friends and family about your excessive Internet use.** It is critical for you to avoid secrecy about your Internet use. Keeping the amount of time you spend online a secret can contribute to the experience of Internet addiction. The hallmarks of any addictive behavior are *shame, secrecy,* and *isolation.* Shame associated with secrecy and continued isolation contributes to the ongoing problem. Tell your friends and family that you're worried about your Internet use. Telling others offers the potential for support, decreases shame, stops social isolation, and promotes the healing process.

Because all human problems exist in a social context, so must the healing process. Internet abuse and addiction are insidious because *Internet use is a behavior that is typically practiced alone.* The more you use it, the more isolated you become;

the more isolated you become, the greater the likelihood that you'll continue to feel shame and engage in self-defeating, addictive patterns.

If the isolation continues, depression may occur. The more depressed you become, the more likely it is that you will resort to behaviors that artificially elevate your mood, which can restart the addictive process. All addictive behaviors have the capacity to do this: gambling, Internet, drugs, alcohol, shopping, sex, and food can all have a mood-altering effect. The problem is that we tend to *repeat* those behaviors that make us feel good even when they have a cost or consequence, thus creating a repetitious cycle of addiction, shame, isolation, and depression.

6. **Try counseling or psychotherapy to assist you in dealing with the addictive behavior.** At times it's too difficult to break the addictive cycle alone. A psychologist or other trained mental health professional can help you to identify your options. The *support, acceptance,* and *coaching* that a psychologist provides can be of immeasurable help in getting a handle on a difficult behavior pattern. Professional help can often make a difference in starting and maintaining your recovery. Whomever you choose for help should have experience in the treatment of addictions. More importantly, the person you choose to work with should possess the ability to instill confidence in your ability to change. Don't be afraid to ask questions of the psychologist regarding his or her background and experience.

Above all, find a person that you're comfortable with. The psychotherapy relationship is a very personal one, which requires trust, honesty, and openness. Take your time and be careful to find the right doctor or therapist to work with. It will pay off in the long run. You can obtain a referral to a psychologist by contacting your local or state psychological association, which should be listed in the yellow pages. Many associations operate a statewide referral service, which can also be found in the yellow pages. Sometimes your primary physician can offer names of psychologists he or she has worked with in the past.

Sometimes friends and family can also be good resources, based on positive experiences they may have had.

There are times when counseling or therapy isn't enough. These are times when medications may be a useful tool to assist you in your healing. Medications, particularly the SSRIs, which are a type of antidepressant, seem to have fewer side effects, and are therefore better tolerated by people. SSRI stands for *selective serotonin reuptake inhibitor.* They function by increasing the availability of serotonin to the brain, and can be helpful in elevating one's mood and dealing with the compulsivity and stress of breaking the addiction cycle. Whomever you work with can advise you on medications. There are some drugs that may be helpful in reducing cravings and decreasing compulsive feelings as well. Anti-anxiety medications may be useful as well.

7. **Consider a support group.** There are support groups for Internet abuse and addiction. Unfortunately, many of these groups are online and also serve as chat rooms. One person e-mailed me criticizing online support groups, analogizing them to "holding an AA group in a bar." Although I believe he has a point, it would be premature to discard all therapeutic uses of the Internet. There may be some people who can access the Internet in a healthy way and can use the Net to their benefit. However, it does seem contradictory to me to spend *time online* to try to spend *less time online.* However, there is good support and information from these support group sites. If there are no support groups available, you may want to consider starting a support group of your own in your community. I receive many calls from people asking about support groups and there are many more beginning at this point. These groups may also be effective for spouses and family members of Internet addicts, as there can be as much stress for those who love and live with an Internet addict as for the addict themselves.

For example, Jane contacted me after reading about my research on ABCNEWS.com and described an all too common scenario. She went on to explain how her husband had met someone online four years ago and that she felt it had ruined her marriage. She felt she'd lived through it all: lies, cheating, exorbitant phone bills, and verbal abuse. Jane could benefit by having a place to deal with her feelings about living with an Internet addict (not to mention the betrayal she feels from her husband's cyberaffair). To accomplish this, there is probably no better place than a support group with people who have been through the same or similar situation. Jane did find such a group online, and now has the courage to begin changing her life, including leaving her husband. In the Resources section at the back of this book, you'll find information and Web site addresses for support groups, along with suggestions on how to start your own group.

8. **Other traditional support groups, such as Alcoholics Anonymous (AA), Sex Addicts Anonymous (SA), and Gamblers Anonymous (GA), can be useful as well.** The principles of a twelve-step recovery group can be applied to any compulsive behavior interfering with your life. Don't be afraid to use them, and because they're more available than Internet-addiction groups, you can get some needed support right away. No one will judge you if your addiction is different than the focus of the group. Most twelve-step recovery groups provide support and assistance, especially when you're open to it. Some of the support groups that might be helpful include:

   • Alcoholics Anonymous
   • Narcotics Anonymous
   • Alanon (for family and friends)
   • Alateen (for teenagers)
   • Alatot (for children)
   • Co-dependents Anonymous (for friends and loved ones who are living with or involved with an addict)
   • Gamblers Anonymous (this may be the one that is most closely aligned with Internet addiction, due to the similarities between Internet addiction and compulsive gambling)

- Gamanon (for family members and friends of gamblers)
- Sex and Love Addicts Anonymous
- Sexaholics Anonymous
- Sex Addicts Anonymous
- Overeaters Anonymous
- Debtors Anonymous

Each has a common set of qualities, such as: unconditional support, a place to share, a twelve-step recovery plan to follow, and the availability of sponsors to act as mentors in your recovery process. These support groups can offer a sense of community and connection that can be critical in helping you conquer a strong habitual pattern like Internet addiction. Sometimes the act of disclosing to someone (especially someone who has their own addiction) can be very powerful medicine in your recovery process.

9. **Develop new relationships and friendships.** Developing new friendships can expand the inner satisfaction that you experience in your life. Although technology is stimulating, it may not provide the personal/emotional connection that real-time relationships do. Advances in technology create opportunity for new adventures, but they cannot fully duplicate the intimacy of human contact. The computer and the Internet *do* have the capacity to connect you to the world, making the world a smaller place; however, these activities are typically engaged in isolation, and can be socially alienating, which is why it's important that you develop some real-time connections. This is not to say that cyberfriends cannot be real and valuable. But there are limitations to the love, support, and intimacy available online. There may even be detrimental aspects to living your social life online, such as depression and increased social isolation. It may simply come down to the fact that as human beings we have an innate biopsychosocial need to have real human contact.

For example, Joe had developed a problem. He spent so much time online that he had lost contact with all his friends and family. About six months had gone by since he bought his new computer and had gone online. Since that time he was online nearly every day beginning right after work until nearly two A.M. His friends began to complain that they never saw him anymore and that they were worried about Joe. His mother had even called the police on one occasion because she hadn't heard from him for over two weeks and the phone line was busy all the time. She was sure something bad must have happened to him for him to be so unreachable.

Finally, his friends got together and confronted Joe about what he was doing. He was forced to listen to them. After his friends intervened, Joe began to question his addictive Net surfing. He began to cut back. He would go several days without going online, and would only check his e-mail when he had to. He started to go out with his old friends, and he has made some new ones by joining a men's basketball league two nights a week. After a while he hardly missed his cyberfriends, although he would talk to them occasionally when he went online to check his e-mail.

10. **Shorten your Internet sessions.** Because the Internet distorts the passage of time, steps need to be taken to ground the user to the here-and-now. One way to do this is to increase your consciousness of the amount of time that you spend online. This can be accomplished by putting an old-fashioned (preferably analog) alarm clock next to the computer to help you keep track of the time. The clock will act as a positive reminder to help you recognize the reality of passing time and hopefully act as an anchor to your real-time life.

Once you are grounded in earth-time you can potentially make more reasonable decisions regarding time spent on the Net. In addition, try to fill your life with enough real-time activities that you will not have the time to spend so many hours online. If it is too difficult to stop your use at once, then try to slowly reduce the number of hours you spend each week over several weeks, until you have reached your goal. For some of you, the goal may be no time online, while for others it may be a specified (but limited) amount of time each day.

For example, Sally loved the Internet. Besides using it at work all the time, she spent nearly forty hours a week staring at her PC at home. She was beginning to believe that perhaps she loved the Net a bit too much. Sally did not want to stop using the Net, but she did want to try reducing the amount of time that she used it. She began a plan to reduce her use by ten percent a week for nine weeks. By the tenth week she had brought her use down to only four hours a week! Some days Sally did not even turn on the computer, and she didn't feel like she was missing anything; she also replaced her online time with other pleasurable activities, which in Sally's case was reading and mall walking.

11. **Watch your moods and behaviors that may prompt Internet abuse.** Note your boredom as this can prompt you to use the Net. We tend to resort to well-established patterns and coping mechanisms when bored, tired, hungry, or feeling other strong emotions. Loneliness is also a common cause for spending excessive amounts of time online. Watch yourself so as not to make excuses to use the Internet when you don't *have* to. Try to be brutally honest with yourself about whether you *really* need to log on, and try to avoid recreational use of the Net. Ideally, you should abstain from using the Net as much as possible. You can accomplish this by moving the computer to a more public place at home to discourage you from retreating to your familiar pattern of isolated use. Don't buy the fastest cable or DSL modem, which might encourage your use. Try to do your work at a time when you're less likely to abuse the time online (e.g., when you're busy), which may help you set some limits on your use.

12. **Become aware of your rituals and triggers to go online.** A trigger is an *associative link* or *connection* to the addiction pattern. Every addiction creates numerous associations that are formed by behavior rituals (patterns) performed

during the development of the addiction. These rituals become very conditioned to your whole behavior pattern and can serve to kick off the addictive cycle.

If, for example, you tend to log on every night at six P.M. after you've watched the news, then six P.M. and the news become *triggers* to your addiction. In other words, when the trigger occurs it can act as a catalyst for the addiction cycle to start, and once it starts, it's difficult to stop! The key then is to avoid or change some of your patterns, habits, and rituals in order to decrease the likelihood of triggering a relapse when you're trying to quit. Triggers are important to be aware of at all times, and they can affect you quite unconsciously and can be subtle. Sometimes it can be a minor thing that can act as a trigger, so it's critical to be aware of everything that you associate with your Internet use.

For example, to Jimmy, a thirty-four-year old stockbroker, the Net was the most fun he'd ever had. It wasn't long before he was spending most of his free time online. He started calling in sick to his job to spend more time on the Internet. When he did go to work he would spend several hours a day surfing from his terminal on his desk. He was even downloading pornography and saving it on his hard drive. However, he had a scare one day when his friend had gone into his office on a day he had called in sick to use Jimmy's computer. His friend accidentally stumbled onto Jimmy's cache of saved porno files and called Jimmy at home to let him know. Jimmy was mortified and he felt a lot of shame, particularly because his employer had just send out the latest memo on the company's Internet use policy.

His friend gently warned him (and gave him a hard time), but then let it go. Jimmy couldn't let it go. The next day he found a support group for Internet addicts online and went to see a Dr. Stevens, a psychologist who specialized in addiction and worked with several Internet addicts. The first thing Dr. Stevens did was to establish a trigger list in a hierarchical order from most likely to tempt his using to least likely to tempt his use. This list was then fine-tuned to develop a relapse-prevention plan for Jimmy. This plan included developing alternate response strategies for Jimmy to follow when he found himself experiencing a trigger to go online.

Relapse prevention planning is a critical component to any addiction recovery plan; it helps you prepare for any anticipated and some unanticipated triggers that can kick off the addictive cycle.

For Jimmy the triggers were fairly straightforward. When he got bored, lonely, tired, or angry he tended to go online. With his new relapse prevention plan, Jimmy was able to identify when certain emotions were present and to take steps to avoid acting out and going online in his usual manner. At times triggers can be completely unexpected, so it is important to have some help in identifying them. It's difficult to be completely objective and honest with yourself when you may still be in denial to some degree.

13. **Utilize spirituality as a support in making the changes you desire in you're life.** Spirituality can be a great resource for people. This doesn't have to just be about God or organized religion, but rather the ability to connect with a higher sense of self or a power in the universe. For some people, this is accomplished through God or organized religion, for others prayer, meditation, martial arts, exercise, the outdoors, art, music, or poetry can serve to enliven their spiritual center. The important part is to be able to connect with your inner self, to expand that connection outward toward others, and to utilize that connection as a resource in your recovery. The nurturing of the soul cannot be overestimated in helping us face adversity and to experience inner growth.

6

Cyber-Relating

The New World of Relationships on the Internet

*The Internet is a virtual petri dish
for sexually-related activity.*

Many people wonder what exactly terms such as *cyber-relationship*, *cybersex*, and *cyberaffair* mean. I will attempt in this chapter to define, and hopefully clarify, these for you. I will discuss how such relationships start and end, and offer suggestions on what you can do about the negative effects to your marriage or relationship due to the Internet.

Online Intimacy

Regardless of the terminology, it seems clear that *intimate relationships* (sexual or otherwise) *outside a marriage* can seriously affect the quality of a marriage or other real-time relationships. Intimacy with other people can disrupt a primary relationship, and cyber-relationships on the Net are no exception.

Online intimacy and relationships are not necessarily bad. There are many good things that can come from the ease of relating online. Even cybersex may be seen as a safe alternative to far riskier real-time sexual contact, and may be seen as a safe alternative to cruising in a singles bar. Surfing for love is safe, cost efficient (no transportation costs or bar tabs), and saves energy. E-mail can be a good way to practice social skills, so long as you leave cyberspace sometimes. Socially awkward, shy, or recently divorced/separated people find that the Net can virtually open doors.

The following three e-mails reflect frequent sentiments I received regarding how the Net has helped them socially.

> *Going online has IMPROVED my social life! I've met people with similar interests and then met them in person. This has led to ongoing friendships.*

> *I'm shy in social situations but am more open on the Net, in chat rooms. I'm shy about approaching people at a party or in a large group, for example, but not about talking to people in chat rooms.*

> *Not really the story of addiction, but I wanted to tell the positive story of meeting my fiancee on America Online . . . Compared to some of the bad stories I'm sure you've heard, ours is a good one. We met almost two years ago and we've been together for one and a half years . . . nothing bad has happened. All high points from my view.*

There is some risk to relating in cyberspace. Real-time intimacy implies a personal connection between two or more people. *Intimacy in real life is a three-dimensional experience.* The Net can be a two-dimensional social experience. The Internet is limited in its ability to capture *all of the person* you're communicating with. With the Net, it's difficult to separate *your projection* of who your cyberfriend is, due to the heavy use of fantasy and imagination. Fantasy can be a very powerful aphrodisiac, as most powerful sexual and intimate experiences begin in the mind.

Although you could argue whether cyberintimacy is real or not (and I have hundreds of e-mails from people who attest to the love they've found online), it does seem that people experience *online intimacy* as very real. Often, I'm afraid the fantasy and promise of cyberspace won't live up to reality. Even though you often feel an enhanced sense of intimacy online, it's as yet unclear whether this in fact represents a complete illusion. There is no long-term research on the longevity of online relationships and the experience of intimacy. There is a great deal of anecdotal evidence of marriages and real-time relationships that began online, which *proves the point that many relationships, in order to progress, must leave cyberspace.* Most likely, however, there are some relationships that begin and remain online. There is evidence to suggest that such a relationship possesses intimacy of a sort, but probably not the same type of intimacy as found in real-time relationships. Online, there is *less accountability, greater anonymity,* and *less need for commitment.* Online intimacy may reflect a different type of communication and relationship altogether. Some critics might even suggest that online intimacy is in fact a pseudo-intimacy. In fact, online intimacy may reflect fears of real-time intimacy.

My research seems to suggest that there may be stages of progressive development in cyber-relationships and cybersexuality, which is consistent with other research (Cooper, Scherer, Boies, and Gordon 1999), beginning with the most innocent e-mail to full cybersexual affairs, and eventually real-time affairs. The progression often follows the following course:

- Meeting in a chat room or game/topic site
- Increased frequency of e-mail and/or Instant Messages
- More overt cyberflirting begins
- Development of planned and preset meeting times to speak off-line or meet in private rooms

- Use of private chat rooms for more personal discussion (by this time the sexual innuendo has increased considerably, perhaps escalating to cybersex, where explicit sex acts are discussed as stimulation to reach orgasm)
- Frequent progression toward telephone contact, including phone sex (similar to cybersex, on the telephone)
- A personal meeting, which in up to 31 percent of the cases, results in real-time sexual contact

The previous developmental illustration is by no means exact, but reflects a composite of research, clinical, and e-mail data. The exact progression is likely to vary quite a bit, but will often include most of the stages I've noted.

Sex in Cyberland

Anyone who's used the Internet is probably familiar with the sexually-related features and services available online. Adult Web sites are (as is probably becoming clear by this point) one of the largest current use areas online. There are literally hundreds, perhaps thousands, of sexual Web sites, chat rooms, and live video feed sites. This doesn't even include the frequent *cybersexual liaisons* that occur between people in *private member rooms, public chat rooms,* and through *online personals.* Anyone who uses e-mail is all too familiar with the frequent, annoying, and obtuse invitations for sexual adventure, if you "simply click here."

The proliferation of this sexual-Spam has become an increasing problem of intrusion into our private Internet world. Indeed, the purveyors of adult Web sites have gotten quite sneaky. They often disguise the invitations to their sites to encourage you to sign up for regular access. In many cases, once these sites have your credit card number they may continue charging you even after you no longer wish to receive their service.

The Internet is a perfect launching pad for the exploitation of human sexuality. The combination of instantaneous access, live interaction, anonymity, and easy availability make the Internet a fertile breeding ground for sexual encounters of all kinds. The Net has become a virtual supermarket for all types of sexual experiences, with an unlimited audience of potential consumers. There are numerous cases of people starting adult sites on there own to cash in on the cybersex wave. One e-mail from a person responding to our online study describes such a case:

I don't get into chat very much, but I have a friend who goes online and impersonates a woman to get personal photos of lesbians. He has to tell them his panty hose size (B, he told me!) as a test to get in their little group. You may ask how he found this out (panty hose size)—he asked his wife! I couldn't get into that though. There is so much porn out there. Why bother doing such a scheme to get porn. I have recently met a twenty-five-year-old male who makes one hundred fifty thousand dollars a year with a porn Web site and does it all from his bedroom! I doubt that this guy is the only one who does this!

Sexual Addiction and the Net

I believe that a large number of Internet addicts may actually be sex and relationship addicts as well. In some cases their primary addiction may be sex, and they use the Net for its availability and easy access. In our study it was found that a full 20 percent of Internet addicts felt they could be described as addicted to sex.

The Internet is so sexually alluring to many people that it becomes an easy way to fulfill their sexual desires. Among Internet addicts there's a clear need for an increase in sexually stimulating material to achieve the same degree of satisfaction (31 percent of male Net addicts report this!) and 57 percent admit to flirting online as well. Thirty-eight percent admit to explicit sex talk, with someone online. Thirty-one percent of our addicted research participants admit to having a sexual relationship with someone that they met online! An amazing 37 percent even admit to masturbating while online. All these figures drop dramatically for general Net users, who don't report being addicted to the Internet.

The Oldest Industry Meets the Newest

Sexually-related Web sites seem to be proliferating at exponential rates. Although their growth is slowing, they're everywhere on the Internet. Every day there is another adult site beckoning us with a disguised e-mail solicitation. Recent Senate and FCC hearings regarding the protection of free speech on the Internet were an attempt to address the expansion/intrusion of the sex industry on the Internet. No significant changes were made, but it's clear that our society is struggling to answer some tough questions regarding how "free" free speech should really be online.

This debate is particularly important, as the traditional rules for communication are different on the Internet. The Web was conceived as a place for free and boundless self-expression without censorship or limitations. Even the HTML programming language is designed to be universally accessible and adaptable for universal applications. The idea of limitations and censorship becomes particularly repulsive to many general users of the Internet as a matter of principle.

Sexually-related Adult Sites

Let's review what is actually currently available on the Internet. Sexual sites can be seen in a variety of combinations, ranging from simple photos of individual naked men and women, to examples of fetishism and other bizarre sexual practices. Some of the sites on the Net contain information that's highly unusual and, in some cases, illegal, as in the case of child pornography. In the majority of cases the material provided contains explicit sexual items, with a variety of specialty options for the more discriminating consumer. Typically these services are only available after you enroll in a paid membership and are *not* offered in the free samples.

All that is needed to explore these sites is access to the World Wide Web and, for those with the most explicit material, a credit card. Most Web sites offer free information for introductory purposes in order to tease you into signing up as a member for the "really good stuff." The most explicit photos cannot be seen without this membership, which is set up online by completing a registration form along with your credit card number. The initial sampler may include some text describing the Web site, as well as a few photographs or other visual clips.

Most Web sites present lengthy disclaimers indicating that the material is for adult consumption only and that you must be over twenty-one years old to enter; however, they require no proof. It's highly probable that children and teenagers are lying to gain access to these sites without their parents' knowledge. Unfortunately, with the current state of Internet technology, there's no way to accurately verify the age of users of such information. There are some age-verification programs used, but they are few and far between and not reliable.

Virtually *anyone* with access to the Web can log on to these sites with or without parental supervision. If they provide a credit card number they can order and download the hardest-core material, including live-action videos. My sense is that we're not too far off from requiring a standardized age verification program for any adult Web site. This might involve a code that you can only obtain from a registration process with actual proof of age.

There are several Web screening and filters programs, such as *Net Nanny, CyberTot, Cyberpatrol, Cybersurfer,* and others. However, they are not 100 percent reliable and there are ways to bypass them if you know your way around the computer. For the time being, it seems likely that many children and adolescents will be able to access this information with little or no trouble, and this is of great concern. Often children are more familiar with computers than their parents are and can bypass some of the safeguards with a little effort.

Many of the adult sites will Spam (send unsolicited info) key words that the screening programs cannot detect and there have been numerous cases where children have gained access to sexual material that can traumatize or overstimulate them. The trauma comes from exposure to sexually explicit material before they are psychologically prepared to handle the natural sexual stimulation that occurs. If a child is prematurely stimulated in this way, it can lead to sexual dysfunction, promiscuity, and a potential to develop a sexual addiction.

Our research shows that even with nonaddicts, 46 percent of those surveyed logged on to pornography sites for an average of an hour and a half a week. For Internet addicts the numbers are alarmingly high, with 62 percent viewing adult material for an average of *over fours a week*. This is of particular concern because nearly 30 percent of our eighteen thousand subjects were under twenty-one years old. Because of this I believe younger Internet users will be at considerable risk for developing abuse or addiction problems related to these adult Web sites. Chapter 11 has more detailed suggestions and goes into greater detail on the warning signs surrounding Internet use and children. Also presented in chapter 11 are suggestions a parent can follow to minimize any negative impact on their child's life from the Net.

Some Web sites contain examples of explicit photographs of bestiality and animal sex, as well as another that contained sexual depictions of human defecation, urination, and vomiting. While there are disclaimers and warnings on such sites, this only heightens the curiosity factor for many people, especially a child! Anyone wishing to log on to such sites should be forewarned that they may view information that they would find highly objectionable and potentially disturbing. Again, this is particularly important with regard to children who may purposely or accidentally log on to these sites, as exposure to such explicit and violent material may create a covert sexual abuse experience, in so far as it involves exposure to inappropriate sexually toxic experiences.

Live-Action Video and Cam Sites

One of the latest technological advances in the area of sexuality on the Internet is the advent of live video feeds and cam sites. Sometimes referred to as *real-time* or *streaming video*, these are digitized sexual video images transmitted onto the Web. People logging on to the site pay a fee to view prerecorded or live-action video scenes (generally, of individuals having sex).

True to American ingenuity, the latest improvement is the development of the ability to *direct* the sexual action by offering suggestions and requests via e-mail or telephone. You simply tell them what you would like to see, and the actors will portray your sexual fantasies right there in front of you, live. All you have to do is be prepared to hand over your credit card number to become a pornographic video director. This form of interactive voyeurism couldn't exist without the Internet, and it reflects the potential power this new technology possesses.

Cam sites are a recent innovation, where anyone can purchase an inexpensive video camera that transmits still photos at various intervals on to the web. Some of these sites are run by individuals who portray their daily lives (including sex and nudity), while others are run by professionals who are portraying amateurs to heighten interest and credibility. These sites have met with great popularity because of their "amateur" appeal.

The costs for all of these services vary anywhere from a monthly membership of twenty dollars, on up to one hundred dollars or more per use. In many cases, there's a monthly access fee that allows access to the members-only sessions of these Web sites, which usually contain the more intense sexual material. More customized services are usually a la carte, similar to pay-per-view on cable TV.

Cookies

Anyone logging on to an adult Web site might unwittingly be notifying other adult-related merchants of their interest in the topic by the use of *cookies*. Cookies are like tracking devices. These cookies allow the Web site that is logged on to to track users who are interested in the products that they are selling, and to sell your e-mail address to mailing list companies who will in turn sell your address to other sex sites. When such information is found, these other Web sites will actually e-mail you directly, offering services and products that they think might interest you. This is another prime example of the potential power of the Internet—the ability to selectively track and target your marketing to exactly those people who you know may want your product or service. This represents a revolution in marketing efficiency.

This is also done with other areas of content besides sexuality and is largely responsible for the proliferation of Internet junk mail or Spam that you may find on your e-mail account. In many some cases, these e-mail messages contain hypertext or links to other sites; you need only click on the highlighted letters, which will instantly connect you to their particular Web site with ease. These links or banners are responsible for generating significant revenue for the Web sites, as other sites and advertisers will pay fees to have connections to their Web site if they know you've got the viewers (or eyeballs in Net parlance).

Each new viewer represents a potential new customer, who is prescreened and qualified. You may find that a particular site offers "free" pornographic photos, but also displays the links and banners from other sites. The sites with the greatest number of "hits," or "click-throughs," will tend to attract the greatest number of links and advertisers, as they are guaranteed good exposure to the exact demographic audience that is likely to buy their goods and services.

Future commerce of all types will be directly targetable to specific potential buyers with the marketers having instant access to their computer at home and work. Not only will consumer needs be met, but the advertisers will be able also to focus this marketing on the basis of exact geographic, demographic, and psychographic variables. This is laser-accurate advertising, digital style, and it is going to change the way we buy in the next decade.

It seems clear by most estimates that a large degree of the initial e-commerce on the Internet involved sex. Sex sells and it sells *really* well on the Net. After all the Net is the perfect medium: private, accessible, discreet, and safe. The sale of sex on the Net is losing predominance slowly, as more companies do a greater amount of non-sexual business online.

As more businesses look to the Net, sex sites are losing their economic lead when it comes to electronic commerce. In addition, the high number of charge-backs (where the consumer cancels the transaction through the credit card company) has stifled some of the largest Internet pornography purveyors. Nevertheless, Internet historians (and we're talking a short history here) credit the early commercial viability of the Internet to sex sites, where they proved that the Internet could generate sales in a new and profitable way.

Chat Rooms: The Electronic Bedroom

Web sites and chat rooms are by no means only sexual in nature. However, in reviewing the member activity on the heaviest used chat rooms on most Internet Service Providers (ISP), one gets the sense that many (if not most) of the chat rooms involve sexual innuendo and excessive flirting at a minimum. Our research suggests that among general Internet users, 42 percent use chat rooms and 76 percent use e-mail. Among Internet addicts the use of chat rooms goes up to 57 percent! It seems of those people who are heavy chat room users, a majority engage in flirting or explicit sexual discussions. In other words, there appears to be rampant flirting with frequent direct and indirect references to sex. One user's e-mail speaks to the addictive nature of online chat:

> *When I first got AOL I couldn't get enough of it. I would log on at five P.M. and stay on until two A.M. and I had to get up at four A.M. I was actually addicted. If I met someone online, I would sit there and talk in a chat room until he would get online. My family said it was like I got a fix when I could talk with that person. So if anyone says it's not addicting, it's like saying "I can quit smoking anytime" and those words are like water flowing down hill.*

The Net appears to be well suited to flirting. This may be due, in part, to the anonymity and lack of inhibition that occurs on the Net where expressive freedom allows one to become more flirtatious than one might ordinarily be. There is something about the Net that allows individuals to feel that sense of sexual disinhibition. They are able to utilize sexual language more easily, with less concern about how it sounds. There is something about the safety and anonymity of the Internet that allows people to express him- or herself freely. This phenomenon seems to be contagious, insofar as even in the most innocent-mannered, individuals tend to become more flirtatious than they would be in real-life conversations. It appears to be different than the telephone, although 50 percent of Net addicts and 18 percent of nonaddicted users do contact their e-mail and chat friends by phone.

Chat rooms seem to be simmering with overt sexuality and suggestions thereof. There are countless chat rooms that have names such as *Lusty Babes, Big Ones,* or *Les-Love,* all of which serve to suggest strong sexual themes. Often the information shared in these chat rooms is of questionable truthfulness. We like to pretend while performing on the world's largest stage—the Internet.

It appears that men and women use chat rooms almost equally, and that the degree of flirting and sexual innuendo is about equal among males and females as well. Of course you don't actually know who is a man and who is a woman, although based on our research results, the Internet is being utilized by men about twice as frequently as women at this point. However, statistics seem to show that general Internet use is split nearly 50/50 with sightly more males than females. In many cases, individuals who portray themselves as women are actually men masquerading as such. Because the Internet is completely anonymous you can be anyone you want to be and you can be as many people as you want to be.

There's a great deal of lying that goes on online. Our research indicated that 50 percent of Net addicts lie about some aspect of their life, and 20 percent of general users lie as well. This is the downside of the freedom and anonymity. Your imagination becomes your only limitation and your conscience your only governor. There's nothing like face-to-face interaction to foster honesty, although there's certainly no guarantee there either.

Getting Off Online

Many people use chat rooms as an opportunity to engage in *cybersex* or what I have termed "getting off online." Typically, it involves conversations of a sexual nature ranging from covert and subtle messages of a flirtatious nature to overt discussion geared toward ultimately achieving a sexual release. It seems that in chat rooms people are able to utilize sexual language more easily, with less concern about how it sounds. Among Internet addicts it also involves masturbation about 40 percent of the time, and among general users, about 13 percent masturbate while online, although it's not clear how one can masturbate while typing (at least legibly). It seems there is now a mouse that can be operated with your feet so as to leave your hands free in creating that true multimedia experience!

The chat room phenomenon appears to be growing. It seems probable that a great deal of the addictive potential for the Internet is due to the heavy use of chat rooms and private rooms, as many of the largest ISPs report the heaviest regular use areas in chat rooms.

Personals

Individuals should always exercise extreme caution when meeting people whom they've met over the Net. I have spoken to many people who have indicated that they met over the Net and have established successful and, in some cases, long-lasting personal relationships. However, there are an equal number of horror stories, in which individuals had met people they knew only from the Net and, in some extreme cases, were abducted, raped, or even killed. Remember, on the Internet, you truly are buying a "pig in the poke" and the degree of anonymity creates a safe distance for dishonest as well as honest people! Fortunately, most often such extremes do not occur and the worst news is that the person is a jerk. The end of this chapter presents guidelines to help you assess your new found cyberlove.

The Internet is also a potential boon for *personal ads*. The Net allows you to narrow your search to specific geographic or demographic variables, which allows you to be quite specific in meeting your desires. Again, for some of the same reasons previously noted, personal ads lend themselves to the Internet medium. The Internet allows for a larger potential audience and easier access to people than would ordinarily be available. Our research survey is a case in point. We received over eighteen thousand responses in less than two weeks! There is no communications medium on earth that can reproduce those results for the same cost.

There are the stories that you've probably heard in the media of people who met in chat rooms and fell hopelessly in love and lived happily ever. Due to accelerated intimacy there are also those stories where your cyberprince was actually a virtual frog! There are numerous instances where people meet in an interest or topic room and begin a relationship based on mutual interests. This is no different than meeting someone at a class or activity where you share a common interest. Many of these topic rooms have personal ads as a feature of that room or service, which again is the electronic equivalent of meeting at, say, a Sierra club meeting. The topic rooms may certainly include nonsexual areas, but even those can seem to have a flirtatious flavor. The followings examples are representative of the hundreds of e-mails I received regarding reasonable healthy love online:

> *We met online and immediately fell in love. We're currently living together, engaged to be married, and happier than ever in our lives.*

> *In the early days of the Internet, before the World Wide Web, there were Bulletin Board Services (BBS) that are similar to the chat rooms of the Web. Rather than clicking on links and using Java, we had to telnet into a server and check for new messages. I was on it constantly. I was a sophomore in college and, after a promising freshman year, I was spiraling down the vortex of Internet addiction. I stopped going to classes, I stopped doing homework, and I pretty much stopped sleeping. When I wasn't online, I was running up huge phone bills talking to people that I met online from all over the country (the campus provided a free Internet link).*

> *Most of my time was spent searching for girls who would feed my ego and excite me sexually. Needless to say, there were plenty of girls who became a lot less conservative online. Finally, after about a year and a half of searching and many long distance relationships (LDRs), I found a girl close by and we have a strong and loving relationship. In May we're to be married. Because of her, I no longer needed the Internet to feed my desires, imagination, and intelligence. I shifted the focus of my life toward my college education. I have since graduated and got a very good job with a well-known international company. Looking back on that period in my life, I'm disappointed at my lack of will and discipline. However, I am glad that I met my future wife and that is also how I learned to type.*

I met my husband on a chatline. It was my first time on this particular line. We talked about dating . . . or lack thereof, how a good companion is hard to find. We shared stories. It turned out that I was telnetting from a small town that he used to live in, before he was relocated three hours away. He offered to take me out to dinner that folowing weekend, since it was his birthday and he knew of a good restaurant in the area. I don't think either of us were looking for love at that moment, but when we met, I didn't want to say good-bye.

Most Internet relationships go through phases—send pictures, exchange e-mail, phone calls, letters, etc., etc. Somehow, I met him online on a Thursday night, and irl (in real life) the following Sunday. It never happens like that. I am lucky he wasn't a psycho, wacko, or any other dysfunctional person. Three years later we married. And if it wasn't for the Internet, I wouldn't have met my Michael. The Internet is a beautiful thing. It's when it's abused that it becomes ruined.

An online relationship often develops rapidly and may move to a room where they may engage in personal discussion. If someone wishes to have cybersex, they can actually retire to the equivalent of an *electronic bedroom.* These are private chat rooms, where one can privately engage in cybersex with no one viewing the conversation.

Back to personal ads. In personals, any individual can answer an ad and, if the listing individual is interested, phone numbers can be exchanged, often culminating in a real-time meeting. This in essence is no different than how it works in newspapers and magazines, except online personals can be more directly targeted to specific interest groups and demographics.

You should, however, be aware of the fact that the Internet is a completely anonymous medium and not entirely safe. Many of the individuals on the Internet are likely to be lying about some aspect of him- or herself, often including their own sexual identity or other personal circumstances. In some cases our survey showed rates as high as 50 percent for Net addicts!

There are an endless number of cases where people were not who they said they were, and this is often found out after meeting and having a sexual encounter. I was recently told of a case in which a woman, who lived in Chicago, was conversing online and met a man who flew in from Hawaii to see her. They spent a week together and then he disappeared, without a trace! God only knows what his real story was. Stories such as this are not unusual.

Adult Catalogs

The Internet is well suited to the development of virtual shopping. And what product is better suited to online purchase than sexual material? Every sexual product imaginable is available online and there are no embarrassing catalogs to be found at home. There are fewer expenses for the retailer and less inventory to stock. Adult online shopping is only one aspect of what is bound to be a multibillion dollar online shopping industry. I will elaborate when talking about compulsive e-shopping in chapter 8. Again you should exercise caution regarding your child's access to online catalogs because retailers are not likely to require absolute proof or verify age and identity of the purchaser. There is new technology in development that will be able to accurately identify all consumers online utilizing certain codes and preset databases, but this is not in wide use at this time. So, *caveat emptor*.

What You Can Do: Personal Guidelines for Love Online

The following guidelines apply to answering all personal ads, but have particular importance for online personals. Clearly, there are good people on the Net. After all, *you're* online and you're a good person! However, the Net is also a perfect medium for devious and mentally ill individuals to take advantage of unsuspecting victims. Be cautious to not count yourself among other victims.

- If you intend to have a personal contact with somebody you met on the Net, do so in a *public place*.
- Remember most people lie on the Net about *something*.
- Meet during the day, preferably in a busy or crowded area.
- Find out more about the person—verify their information from other sources. Don't be afraid to call references and friend of his or hers.
- Ask direct questions. Don't be afraid of insulting the person; if they're insulted then run the other way, because they probably have something to hide.
- Never, under any circumstances, give out your real name, phone number, or address on the Internet without having a sense of who you are providing it to. Remember, if they really want to, other people can see everything that appears online that isn't encrypted.
- Be specific about your personality and what you want in your ad. Resist the temptation toward being so flirtatious that it clouds your better judgement, or doesn't communicate what you *really* want.

Cybersex

A major phenomenon that has occurred on the Internet is the occurrence of online affairs. I have treated and interviewed numerous individuals who've had online and real-time sex outside of their marriage or primary relationship that in *all* cases started as simple cyberflirting. Often they report tremendous excitement in their cybersexual encounters, which are then typically repeated.

A common question that people have is whether or not an online affair is cheating. The answer to this question is somewhat complex; however, I've distilled it down to a simple formula: *Any time you spend a significant amount of intimate time with another person outside your primary relationship, you may be breaching intimacy rules in your relationship.* It's a personal decision in each relationship whether spending time online and having cybersex are a breach of the relationship contract. Our research does demonstrate, though, that for those who use the Internet addictively, online cybersex frequently extends from cyberspace to the bedroom!

Assess Your Online Flirtation

If you think that your involvement in online sexual interactions may be crossing the line of "acceptability" in your relationship, it's time to take an honest look at your behavior. You might start by asking yourself if your spouse would be upset about your spending many hours a night on the telephone or computer talking to somebody while using sexually suggestive language. If the answer were yes, then they probably would have the same discomfort with your using the Internet in the same manner. It's *not* the medium of communication that's relevant here; it's the effect that *such a detour from your primary relationship can have.* If your spending many hours of the day or night having cybersex, or flirting, you *cannot* have time for those same behaviors within your primary relationship.

The latter part of this chapter will offer more detailed suggestions on how to address these issues in your marriage. There are undoubtedly many people who aren't addicted and who occasionally flirt while online (about 22 percent of general users report cyberflirting). There's probably little harm in this, provided it doesn't interfere with your marriage or relationship. This type of cyberflirting is similar to flirting that goes on at work (barring any sexual harassment issues) and is a natural part of human interaction. However, one should always be mindful of the possible misinterpretation that flirting can have. This is especially true online as you're missing some of the more typical social cues that reinforce social boundaries and imply clear limits.

Cyberflirting: How Harmful Is It?

Many individuals have stated that cybersex and online flirting is always harmful to a real-time relationship. Whether or not this is true, there are clearly some unique factors that make cyberflirting different than real-time flirting. In normal human flirtation, there's typically an implicit, and sometimes explicit, boundary. The boundary states that this flirtatious behavior is pleasant but that it has a clear limit. It is often understood that we may engage in casual flirtatious language, share a glance, make a sexual joke, or tease each other in a provocative manner, but that this is as far as it will go.

Most of these cues are a complex combination of verbal and nonverbal communications, many of which, are not easily expressed on the Internet. Innuendo, exclamation, verbal punctuation, facial gestures, and intonation are all absent on the Net. Combine these factors with the ease of availability, anonymity, and the disinhibition that occurs on the Net, and you have fertile ground for an intensely flirtatious experience without the boundaries found in real-time interaction. All this occurs without of the normal social cues that promote reasonable boundaries. People can easily become carried away experiencing and expressing strong sexual emotion.

It's Easy to Get Carried Away

There have been numerous cases in which people started out on the Net only for the purposes of engaging in casual conversation that unintentionally ended up being highly sexual in nature. In addition, because of the accelerated intimacy that they experience, these people became more involved, more rapidly, then they ever intended. People often report that they experienced levels of intimacy and self-disclosure that were unparalleled in their real-life relationships! Needless to say, this can be highly problematic to your marriage or relationship.

Again, because of accelerated intimacy and disinhibition, people will share information with their Net mate that they wouldn't ordinarily share in their real-time relationship. This can represent a potential significant threat to any primary relationship or marriage. The relaxed conversation style, combined with the sexual themes that often appear in Internet communication, offer serious competition to sometimes mundane real life. After all, how can everyday life compete with the intense, uninhibited excitement of relationships online?

If you want to assess your dependence on an online relationship, or gauge its seriousness, consider discontinuing the online relationship. If that relationship has become a significant one, it will be a difficult break to make. You are experiencing a similar scenario that people undergo when assessing an actual affair—that is, when people address the issues of the *marriage* versus the *affair*. To some extent, however, you will always be comparing a fantasy to real life, which is a tough comparison.

Real-time Marriage Counseling Can be Very Helpful

I often use marital counseling with couples to address the aspects that they're missing in their relationships. It is frequently the more deep-seated issues within a marriage that cause the online affair to begin with. It's difficult to isolate the impact that cybersex may have on a relationship as the effects can be a symptom of other problems. However, it does seems clear that anytime you consistently remove physical or emotional energy from a marriage there has to be a negative effect. How and where that energy is transferred is less relevant, be it work, sports, or the Internet. What does seem to be critical is the fact that intimacy cannot be divided effectively between real-time living and the Internet.

What If You're Involved with a Nethead?

The time that someone spends on the Net may not be recognized as a problem for the Nethead. They may view the time they spend (or relationships they develop) as very significant, but "separate from their real life." This is often the rationale I hear when a problem arises. So significant are the cyber-relationships that they may feel more real to the Nethead than real-time contact.

There is a tendency among those involved with Netheads to dismiss cyber-relationships as less real because they're not personal, and therefore less threatening. This is a potential mistake, for many of these relationships prove to be quite significant in a Nethead's life, and 31 percent of the time cyber-relationships become real-time sexual ones! This is more likely for Internet addicts and heavy Internet users, but even for moderate users this occurs 14 percent of the time! If you notice a cyber-relationship developing, confront your significant other. I receive numerous calls and e-mails from people who are struggling with their loved ones' use or abuse of the Internet; often, they have seen the pattern grow from an initial interest to an obsession, but never said anything until it reached near epidemic proportions.

The power of the Internet and human sexuality shouldn't be taken lightly. Although Netheads are involved in other areas of the Internet, there's clearly a significant sexual component for Internet addicts as evidenced by very high percentages of chat room, e-mail, and Web surfing involving sexual content. There is great potential in this new communications medium, but this power needs to be recognized and understood before we can render it harmless. Because this newest mode of interaction is here to stay, we need to recognize it for the wonderful but complex form of human communication it is.

7

Chatting or Cheating

Crossing the Line, Online

Love hath no boundary in cyberspace.

There is perhaps no easier place to start a relationship than on the Internet. For that same reason there's probably no easier place to have an affair than online. Most people I've seen in my practice who were abusing their use of the Internet were involved in either cybersex, online affairs, or real-time affairs that began online. It seems that the combination of feeling unreserved, nameless, and easily flirtatious produces a potent emotional romantic experience for many Netheads.

Research figures show that a large percentage of Net users pursue their online contacts in the real world. Eighteen percent of nonaddicted Net users extended the reach of the World

Wide Web to the telephone, with a close 17 percent admitting to meeting those they contacted online, and approximately 13 percent admitted to extending cybersex to the real thing. For Net addicts the numbers jump to 50, 44, and 31 percent respectively. Because there really is no substitute for real sex and even the power of an Internet experience does not suffice, most Netheads eventually will "reach out and touch someone."

The powerful Internet experience even extends to masturbation, with nearly 38 percent of addicts surveyed admitting to doing so while online. It isn't clear whether or not masturbation occurs in private rooms, during cybersex, or from viewing pornography on the Net. The percentage is far greater among male Net addicts (42 percent) than female Net addicts (25 percent), and is almost nonexistent among nonaddicted female Internet users. Nonaddicted males will masturbate while online (16 percent), which implies that some online masturbation is done while viewing pornography, as opposed to while relating to an actual person during cybersex. Our research also suggests that approximately 57 percent of Internet addicts flirt online, and an amazing 75 percent of Internet addicts experience intense feelings of intimacy while online. This intimacy presumably occurs during communications with others via chat and e-mail. Even 38 percent of nonaddicted Net users report feeling intense intimacy! Perhaps these results are in part due to the fact that people felt much freer to express themselves on the Net than in their real-time lives, again, because of the disinhibition, immediacy, and anonymity.

Laura, a thirty-six-year-old executive manager, describes the process by her experience:

> *Within my first week of being online I explored a chat room and met someone. Our first conversation was me trying to aid him in his marital problems. Please keep in mind I have never had any problems on a social basis. I'm very open in life and extremely outgoing. We talked for three hours the first night we met. As time went by we chatted on many occasions. We did grow to like each other. We traded various files and jokes*

with each other. We got to know about each other's lives and families. We began to form a good friendship on the Net. We were there to offer each other advice when needed. After five months of continual e-mail correspondence, we both discovered we were thinking of each other more and more throughout the day.

I am a very analytical person by nature. At first I thought this must be one of those online fantasy things. I couldn't figure out why I was thinking of him so much throughout the day. Again I thought my marriage was a good one. I thought my life was fulfilled. So if that is the case, why was I beginning to become infatuated with this man who I have never even met? He also informed me of his thoughts being of me throughout his day. Our friendship caught fire as they would say, and as time went on, we talked more and more to each other online and our feelings were growing stronger for each other. We sent each other pics of ourselves and we took our relationship to an online sexual nature. It took me two months of feeling like I was in love with this man before I figured out why it was taking place. Along with our common interests, and our common viewpoints on many various things in life, we became very caring and loving towards each other.

Many people find it easy to start up a relationship in a chat room, where each new faceless, nameless cyberfriend offers the promise of an exciting encounter without the inherent risks of blind dates. After all, there is no risk if all you do is converse online, and there's no concern about how you appear. In fact, it seems that much of the attraction of the chat and e-mail side of the Internet is that you can relate in an intimate way without physical appearance hindering you; this is especially helpful for people who are homebound or who feel self-conscious about how they look. If you have social fears or are shy, the Internet affords an opportunity to relate on comfortable ground. Conversing online removes many of the social barriers that are often deeply felt by people. I have received numerous e-mails extolling the virtue of the Internet's ability to soften the blows of real-time social contact. For some people this can change their life in positive ways. All you have to know is how to type fast enough (which can put a damper on your conversation if you type as slow as I do). Perhaps it is best described by Sam, a senior at a large university, whose comments reflect hundreds I received by e-mail while conducting my research.

> *I am so damn sociable . . . the Net is like a party at my finger-tips . . . a party that is always going on . . . whenever I choose to join it. I chat with a certain group of friends almost every night . . . we are all around thirtyish and married and enjoy each other's company and sense of humor . . . it's a relaxation thing for us . . . (my hubby loves it . . . it frees up the TV for him to watch SPORTS and more sports!) (Laughing)! Chat addict? Most definitely! The Net taking over my life? No way! I still maintain a healthy happy lifestyle in the real world with real-world friends, a marriage, and a job. I can sincerely say I have made some great friendships over the Net that I wouldn't have made otherwise due to geographical distances. Virtual friendships I cherish as much as my real-world friendships.*

There are numerous stories of people who report significant benefit from their cyber social life. There is little doubt the Web offers social connection and opportunity that are unavailable in real-time living. For some people, however, there may be a negative effect from spending so much time in isolation from real-time companionship. Social isolation can occur on- or off-line, but excessive time online may contribute to further removal from real-time social interaction. One self-defined Internet addict described the social aspects of the Net as "a blessing and a curse." Here she states:

> *I was once addicted to the Internet so much until at times I barely even slept. I hardly ever ate, subsequently losing many, many pounds. My spouse was on an extended assignment in another country, and the Internet and chat were just about my only means of social interaction. It was a blessing and a curse all rolled into one. Yes it is very addicting. I don't go into the*

chat rooms anymore now but I still love surfing the net. I have made serveral very, very good friends through chat and still talk to them several times a month by phone.

The Internet can build certain social skills, but I question whether it erodes other important interpersonal skills. Just as in other forms of addiction, the "drug" starts out as a solution, only to later become a new and more insidious problem. There are many stories of those who felt they became carried away with their cyber social life. One such man e-mailed me with his words of hard-earned advice.

These days I have ICQ, AIM (the two are real-time messaging programs), my own Web page, and a circle of Net friends. I'm still on a lot, but not as often. I'm a little more responsible about the time I spend online now, since I have to juggle studies and a newly-discovered social life. Part of the reason I kept online so often was because I felt very isolated in RL (real life). I don't feel as bad about my social situation more, and I spend less time online and more time with my real-life friends. Not that my Net friends are bad people, of course. It's just not the same because you're not really talking to them face to face.

My advice for junkies? Make some real-life friends and stick with them. Spend time with them and appreciate the "analog" way of life. It's almost like the difference between LPs and CDs. CDs are newer and sound better, but LPs will never really die. Net life can be good, even to the point where it seems better than real life. Real life, however, will always be there. Might as well live it, right?

Is it Chatting or Cheating?

I was recently interviewed for a radio show where I was asked whether cybersex and online relationships constituted an affair. After all, there is no *physical* contact, and doesn't that constitute an affair? There was considerable controversy on the show as to whether engaging in cyberflirting and cybersex represented being unfaithful to one's spouse. One talk show I appeared on had a guest who felt that online cybersex was in fact good for a marriage, and that it added spice to the real-time boredom of relationships and several people in the audience supported this. She did not see it as a violation of the marital contract, as sex did not "technically" occur. Most people did feel that it was a breach of the marital contract while a few others felt it was simply good clean fun, representing a mild harmless diversion. Little or no attention was given to the breach of intimacy that can occur when one spouse places too much time and energy into something (let alone someone) outside the marriage! The fact is, the truth may have more to do with personal values and morals than a technical definition of what constitutes an affair. Suffice it to say that if it causes no harm to your relationship (which seems unlikely if done consistently), more power to you!

We already know that the Internet is widely used for chat rooms and e-mail. A recent study done at Carnagie Mellon University found that Internet users who spend a lot of time in chat rooms and e-mailing are slightly more likely to experience depression, isolation, and loneliness (Kraut, Patterson, Lundmark, Kiesler, et al. 1998). Now the question is how to balance real-time social contact with the time you spend online.

What Is Cybersex?

There is considerable disagreement as to the exact definition of cybersex, but for our purposes let us define it as follows: Cybersex, or cybering, refers to *engaging in consensual and explicit sexual discussions with the main objective of achieving sexual arousal and/or orgasm*. It's probably not unlike phone sex except the communication is typewritten in cybersex. Many cybersurfers feel that spending time online flirting, cybering, or masturbating shouldn't have a negative impact on their personal relationships, as they're totally separate. This issue seems to encompass a wide range of behaviors including, but not limited to, answering personals, chat rooms, IM/ICQ cam sites, private member rooms, e-mail, cyberflirting with sexual innuendo, actual sex talk with the goal of orgasm, phone sex, and in-person sexual encounters. Sexual encounters can even extend to more kinky forms of sex such as S&M (sadism and masochism), bondage and discipline, along with a variety of other assorted flavors of human sexuality. Because sexual contact is so easy online, the potential for Internet addiction is increased significantly.

Easy access makes sexual addiction more probable online than through other mediums (Cooper, Scherer, Boles, and Gordon 1999). It's not known, however, whether sexual activity on the Net produces Internet addiction or simply contributes to it. It's likely that many people are addicted to other aspects of the Internet, which is supported in our research by the fact that less than half of the Internet addicts surveyed engage in cybersex, and less than one-third had real-time sex with someone they met online. I've seen numerous patients in my practice who had a mild problem with compulsive/addictive sexual behavior with pornography or masturbation who then became seriously addicted to adult Web sites.

This problem is further complicated when a spouse or loved one finds out. Often he or she suspects something is going on, just as in a real-time affair, but finds it hard to believe that their significant other can be so involved with a Web site or someone they met on the computer! He or she typically cannot understand the nature of cybersex or online affairs, especially when it comes to the power of instantaneous gratification of the Internet.

There is even new software that has been developed to help people have cybersex and cyberaffairs. It *electronically hides* your communications so they cannot be retrieved by your suspicious spouse. But, before you get too excited, there is also *other* software that allows a suspicious spouse to track and retrieve every keystroke made by their unsuspecting mate! All's fair in love and the Web.

Sexual Addictions

Sexual addiction, whether online or live, *is the compulsive repetition of certain sexual behaviors, which tend to eventually produce negative consequences in one's life.* Sexual addicts, of which the Internet has many, are typically in denial about their problem, which is further compounded by the fact that the computer seems so innocuous and harmless. While an Internet user or addict may often see their behavior as harmless, it may be viewed by their loved one as being unfaithful to the marriage or relationship. Often this compulsive behavior escalates to proportions that are disruptive to all concerned.

The Stages of Cybersexuality

Often the process starts out rather innocently. The following list is a sample progression for involvement in cybersex, online affairs, and real-time sexual encounters. There is no typical situation or reason that it occurs, but I suspect that difficulties in a marriage or relationship plant the seeds for the affair to take root. This list is based on findings from both my practice and our research on Internet addiction.

- *Simply surfing.* People often start out simply surfing the Net and enjoying the whole experience of looking around.
- *Instant messages.* Getting into chat rooms often follows, which is typically where someone IMs (instant messages) you. It is the virtual equivalent of a knock at your door. It can be exciting, like a new friend coming to see you.
- *E-mail.* Often the IMs fizzle, but sometimes you hit it off with someone and you begin to e-mail, or enter a private electronic bedroom I mentioned.
- *Chat rooms and private rooms.* Relationships can also begin in the chat rooms (similar experience to real-time bar hopping), which are often organized around social

or veiled sexual themes. From here you may also meet the cyberlover of your dreams and off you go to the private room to do what you will.

- *Phone calls.* In most cases where actual sex occurs, the meetings were preceded by phone calls. The Net, with its typed interface, can only go so far and almost invariably must lead to verbal contact.
- *Going all the way.* Private room activities vary, but it often involves at least some serious flirting on up to cybersex where a typed form of sexual relations occurs (along with many exclamation marks!). About 15 percent of Net users have cybersex and online affairs, but that number really shoots up when the person is addicted to the Net—to 43 percent!

It's in the chat rooms that many relationships seem to flourish. They may start out innocently enough, simply talking online. Sometimes the conversation becomes more personal and people begin to feel more intimate with their cyberfriend. The *accelerated intimacy* that people feel online is often the fuel for cyberaffairs and real-time sexual experiences that begin on the Net. Combine this intense intimacy, the disinhibition, and the power of the imagination that occurs online and you have a very potent sexual experience. This intense experience often dwarfs normal relationships by comparison. One cybersex devotee describes it aptly:

Veronica is a forty-three-year-old professional with a college and graduate degree. She notes that when she is not at work in the human service field, she is online. She describes the Net as "her major recreational activity," logging on two to three hours per day. She feels that time passes quickly when online and that her family thinks she has a problem, which she disagrees with.

Veronica admits that she spends a lot of time in sexually-related chat rooms having cybersex. She describes having cybersex most times she's online, and masturbates while doing this at least one to two times a week. She describes her first online sexual experience as "honest," as she was being accepted for who she was. Veronica feels that cybersex is a great opportunity for her; the only problem is her husband!

Veronica did not see her cybersex habit as a problem, but her husband clearly did. When he found Veronica's e-mail transcripts, he felt as though he actually caught his wife in bed with a man. It didn't matter to him that it was a virtual man that his wife was intimate with. This issue has caused a considerable rift in their marriage. Veronica still does not wish to give up her cybersex partners! She feels that they are her business and that it isn't cheating. Her husband obviously doesn't agree.

Some people have a lot of trouble integrating their time online with their real-time life. Sometimes, as with the women in the following story, they allow the cybersexual encounter to cloud their reason and make rash judgments that affect other people.

The story is not my story, but that of my wife. She will not admit that she is addicted to the Internet chat rooms. Her addiction has almost ruined our marriage beyond reconciliation. Several months ago she began to frequent the Ancient Sites, e.g., chat rooms. The duration of the time spent began with a couple of hours, which has now turned into approximately eighteen to twenty hours a day, seven days a week. She was looking for "intelligent" conversation, so she says. What an oxymoron, there are few intellects on the Web . . . in chat rooms. She became vulnerable to the flattery of the men seeking sexual conquests.

Over the last eight to ten months, she has committed adultery (in her heart) in the chat rooms and subsequently by phone (nearly two thousand dollars in phone bills), with at least six different men. She can't resist leading them into inappropriate relationships. She is preoccupied with them when she is away from the computer screen. Ironically, she can't carry on an intelligent conversation in "real" life because of her preoccupation with the relationships developed in the chat rooms.

Recently, she secretly bought an airline ticket (from the Nether-
lands to Kansas City, Mo.) for her online lover and met him in
Kansas and committed actual adultery . . . real body contact.
We have two small children, a boy four and a girl who is two.
My wife doesn't do housework, prepare meals, and will not
return phone calls from non-Internet friends. She admits what
she's doing is wrong, but is willing to risk her children just to
stay in front of the computer screen viewing at least three to
four chat rooms at once, with five to six people at any one
time. I think it's more than an addiction, it's an illness of the
mind.

The news is filled with countless stories of Internet
romance disasters. Often these stories are about broken marriages but they're also about people whose whole lives have
become unmanageable, such as the woman's addictive behavior just described. I've heard numerous stories of personal disasters, such as contracted illnesses, loss of custody, loss of jobs,
and financial ruin due to Internet addicted sex and relationships. Not all stories end this way, as there are many happy
endings that people have sent to me. There is no problem with
two single people meeting online and hitting it off, but that is
not what always happens.

Why Are Cyberfriends So Attractive?

About 36 percent of our survey participants were married. Many reported relationship problems due to their online
use and it seems clear that even innocent cyberflirting can
often (31 percent for Internet addicts) escalate to real-time
romance, and herein lies the issue at hand. As we discussed, in
real-life flirting there are implied nonverbal cues that set
boundaries for flirting. You always know via a glance or other
subtle cue where the limits are. On the Internet there are no
such cues. This explains in part why flirting occurs so readily
online and why people seem so free to express their sexual
feelings. Although many would argue that there's no harm in

flirting, there is harm to your real relationship when significant time and energy are placed elsewhere. Internet addicts spend an average of almost nine hours a day involved with their online partners when in the throes of their addiction.

The whole cybersexual encounter becomes a prolonged seduction, where excitement builds to a point where only real-time sex will do the trick. Not saying that all people who chat online will have sex with their cyberfriends, although our research suggests that about 39 percent of female and 26 percent of male Internet addicts will have sex with an online partner! There's no difference seen in our research between nonaddicted males and females with regards to developing sexual relationships; they both report having sex about 13 percent of the time.

Although there are a variety of reasons why so many people seem captivated by online sex, it does seem abundantly clear that it's easy to cross the line, online! In addition it appears that there's a strong relationship between online cyberaffairs and the continuation of those relationships to real-life sexual encounters. If you have had *no* cybersex online it seems *less likely* that you'll have a sexual relationship with someone you meet online, as only 6 percent of those surveyed had no cybersex, but then went on to have real-time sex!

Although our research represents only one study of nearly eighteen thousand people, the implications of these results seem obvious. You're probably much more likely to have a real-time affair if you engage in online cybersex, so the moral is don't play with bees if you don't want to get stung!

So what can you do if you find yourself lighting up a cigarette after you log off your computer and you're real-time love life is off-line? If you believe you're spending more time playing with your keyboard than your mate, then you may have a problem. Even if you don't feel you have a problem, you're mate might think so and this can become serious for your relationship. If you feel you're becoming too dependent upon your computer for your romantic and sexual release, consider the following step-by-step plan to regain your *human sexuality*.

What You Can Do: Ten Steps to Kick the Cybersex Habit

Step 1. *Admit to yourself that you may have a problem with your Internet behavior when it comes to sex.* The act of "making room" within *you* for this possibility, creates the potential for change to occur. I cannot overstate the importance of this step in your recovery.

Step 2. *Create a written list of the specific behaviors you are uncomfortable with.* List those things you do online that may be out of control. If you're logging on to adult Web sites, spending too much time in chat rooms, engaging in cybersex, or having a real-time affair with someone you met online, identify which you would like to change. Be specific. Don't leave out the details and don't be afraid to be honest with yourself. Then write those online behaviors down on a two column "change list." In one column state everything you will gain and lose if you *do* change, and in the second column write what you will gain and lose if you *don't* change. Look at that list every day. Post it where you can easily view it if possible.

Step 3. *Develop a daily behavior list.* Pick some specific behavior you will *do differently every day* even if it represents a small change. You want to begin to create a momentum of change so it can spread to other behaviors and eventually to your whole pattern. Do not give up. Stay with it. This is how all change occurs.

Step 4. *Identify your bottom-line behaviors.* The next step is to decide what you absolutely *have to change* and what you will *not tolerate* doing any longer. For example: You may wish to discontinue viewing adult Web sites; if so, then that would be your bottom-line goal. You must decide on what exactly you will no longer do. It has to be very clear so there is no room for questioning or changing the goal at the last minute.

Step 5. *Nothing new can happen if you don't replace old patterns with new behaviors.* Make room for new actions in your romantic life. Try to change even small things that can start the process of change. For example, take your spouse out for dinner, go for a walk, try to recreate a feeling of intimacy and quality that can begin to *compete* with the intimacy you feel you're experiencing in your online life.

Step 6. *Create a faux online life.* Start by sending a letter to your spouse (either snail mail or e-mail will do). In that letter begin to share with your mate something you've never revealed to them before. Try to slowly introduce some elements of sexual innuendo and flirtation; take small risks and chances by expressing something you've not shared previously. The idea is to introduce an element of the disinhibition and intimacy that so many people report in their online love relationships. It's difficult to compete with cybersex when cyberlife feels so much more exciting. This exercise attempts to capture some of that excitement in your real-time life!

Step 7. *Begin to wean yourself from online relationships.* Try to limit your time online. Use a *timer* or *clock* near your computer. Remember, there is a significant *time distortion* that occurs when online, so there is a need to reintroduce real-life time. Be more aware of how much time you're online. The more you're conscious of this, the greater effect it will have. This helps break the denial. Start to say good-bye to people you met online, and take stock of whether or not they've added to the quality of your life. Start telling your cyberfriends and lovers the *truth* about you and your situation. Remember many people lie online (LOL should really stand for Lie Online, not Laugh Online), and if people knew the truth about things, they might be less likely to continue to have frequent romances online.

Step 8. *Start to go out with other couples.* Spend time with couples whose relationships you admire. Talk to those couples. Ask them what they do that improves the quality of their intimate life. Talk to others. Go on a quest to find out what works, and don't stop until you find it, and then never stop again because a good relationship is always a *process* not an *outcome*.

Step 9. *Remember that sex and intimacy are not the same.* If you have problems in the sex department, that usually means that there are deeper emotional concerns that should be addressed. The biggest of which usually involves communication. Spending quality time together and really communicating is essential. Set aside ten minutes a night for each of you to talk to the other. While your loved one talks, you listen. Don't interrupt. Do not interpret, and above all don't spend the time just preparing your response. Simply listen. At the end of your significant other's talking, you should paraphrase back what they said and ask them if you got it correct. Listen again to the feedback on how you did and try not to be defensive. Remember, the exercise is designed to help, so stay with it. The whole procedure should be repeated with the roles reversed. It may feel silly, but it works.

Step 10. *Consider marriage counseling or psychotherapy with a psychologist or other trained mental health professional.* It would very helpful if they have experience with the Internet as well as with marital counseling and human sexuality. It would also be beneficial if they had experience with addictions and compulsive behavior. Don't get too caught up in credentials though; just try to find somebody recommended to you with whom you feel comfortable. Health insurance may cover some of the cost, but check carefully, as many HMOs don't cover marriage counseling.

The key is to try to change your pattern of behavior. To disrupt the *rituals* you have developed around sex and the Internet. You have to identify any triggers that are likely to remind you to repeat your behavior, and you need to avoid those triggers. For example, not spending time alone in your office with the door closed; you might instead keep the door open, which changes a whole pattern. Habits, especially sexual ones, can be deceptive and the mind's ability to rationalize in order to get pleasure can be quite powerful. Because of this, you must be extremely vigilant as to the possibility of a relapse at any time.

Computer Widows and Widowers of the Net: Rescuing Your Relationship from Virtual Destruction

There is perhaps no area that has been impacted more by the abuse of the Internet than marriage and relationships. Most of the people who have consulted with me in my practice have had problems with Internet addiction and online affairs. Take the case of Mark and Joanne. They are a middle-aged couple married for nearly fifteen years with three healthy children. Both of them are educated professionals and they own a business together. They are financially stable and lead the "good" life by most standards. But something was quite wrong in their marriage, so much so that I received an emergency phone call asking if I could see them as soon as possible.

When I first met Mark and Joanne they appeared to be quite amiable with each other, even happy. However, Mark soon revealed that they were having a real problem in their marriage. What he described to me was a serious and insidious problem. Joanne had been spending an inordinate amount of time online in chat rooms and developed online relationships with several men, some of which were becoming quite intimate.

Joanne had stumbled onto cyberaffairs and cybersex. She and Mark had grown apart as Mark spent more and more time at work. He began to neglect Joanne's emotional needs. The less attention he paid, the more needy Joanne became and the Internet was there to fill the void.

Eventually, Joanne began to fulfill more of her emotional needs with the people she met online, and these relationships began to grow and develop. Joanne was spending several hours a day on her computer. Her story is by no means unusual, as many of the couples that I've interviewed or received e-mails from have indicated that they or their spouse was spending greater amounts of time online, in some cases, ten to twelve hours a day.

The problem of Internet abuse for Mark and Joanne was really secondary to the problems in their marriage. Often the Internet becomes an easy detour for marital problems, as it offers easy access to men and women who are eager and available to talk, and at times, have cybersex or more. Joanne's case seemed to be limited to cyberflirting, but was clearly escalating as the conversations became more intimate. The problem with the Internet is that the combination of *availability, low cost, anonymity,* and *disinhibition* produce a powerful place to run when the home fires begin to wane. The Net is always there, available anytime in your home. It's a friend twenty-four hours a day and, in some marriages, is more reliable than a spouse. No wonder that cyberaffairs and cybersex become significant problems for so many marriages. In some couples I've treated, the Internet proves to be the downfall of the marriage. In many cases (18–50 percent) the cyberaffair progresses to a point where phone and personal contact is made. So what starts out as a simple online friendship can easily become a full-blown affair!

Mark and Joanne were able to work out their marital problems such that the Internet was no longer necessary for Joanne. Joanne followed the ten steps previously listed to help kick her cyberflirting problem. She identified her problematic behaviors and took steps to break the pattern. Her needs that prompted her to spend so much time online were now being fulfilled in her marriage. When I last saw them (after about ten visits) they were happy again with a much-improved relationship.

The Enemy from Within

There are two main areas where the Internet has a negative impact on marriages and relationships. The first develops when a husband or wife stays online for large amounts of time and therefore neglects their relationships, including family, friends, and even children. There have been several cases where an Internet addict has been accused of neglecting their children. The best known was the case of Sandra Hacker (mentioned in chapter 1), who actually lost custody of her children because she was allegedly spending twelve hours or more a day on the Internet while her kids remained unattended.

The time spent away from family and a loved one due to Internet addiction can have a devastating impact on all aspects of a marriage. The following describes the intensity of such a situation.

At the age of forty-two and just having lost my husband, I found that logging on to the Internet was an outlet I used to comfort myself and reduce the pain I was experiencing. There were endless days and nights I found myself online looking for places to visit and people to chat with, to fill the void in my life. I had gone three days straight without sleep, hating to go to my empty bedroom. There were many times that this happened. It was so bad that all I cared about was to feed my twelve-year-old, see that she was taken to school, and get back online as quickly as possible. Not to mention all my family and friends that I lost near complete contact with for a solid year. While ignoring my daughter during this time, she suffered and often lashed out in anger for her mother not being there for her. The bills went unpaid, the house went messy, clothes went unwashed, and worse of all my child was being neglected. Still, I was unable to tear myself away from my computer! I was aware of all the damage I was causing. All I wanted was to surf the Net and chat with people I met there.

I found myself searching to replace the husband I had lost. After fourteen months of this insanity, a close friend alerted a family member of mine as to just how bad the situation was with me. At that time I agreed to be hospitalized and get the help that was well needed. My child agreed with the doctor that her mommy was sick and needed help. Today, I'm glad to say that my daughter has her mommy back. I'm on the road to recovery from my Internet addiction. To all other addicted persons, please seek help before you lose your family and friends as I nearly did. I still enjoy the Net and my many online friends that I met "back in the day," but now at a much more reasonable rate. One must keep a good balance between online time and real time! Thank you for allowing me to share my experiences with you and hope that this may open up the eyes of someone who may not realize the damage their addiction is causing in their life.

She goes on to describe some of the negative consequences of her time online, and offers the caveat that she believes that some of her focus online was a symptom of the loss of her marriage. This is an important point, for the addiction is almost always a response to something lacking in life, and *then it develops a life of its own*. In the case of a marriage with problems, the Internet starts out as a solution, and quickly becomes an addition problem.

There are dozens of e-mails I've received that highlight the negative effects on a relationship as a result of heavy Internet use. That is not to say that there cannot be other reasons for the marital difficulties, as there are many. We know that there are many things that can affect a relationship. Excessive work, verbal or physical abuse, or an addiction, to name a few. The point is that any behavior done at an *extreme* can siphon off the energy required for a healthy relationship. The following example highlights another relationship virtually destroyed by Internet abuse:

My husband of thirteen years got in a Catholic chat room in AOL. At first it was just at night instead of watching TV. Then it became more time, mornings, afternoons and evenings, staying up until six-thirty A.M. He quit doing everything except eating. He was sleeping during the day and chatting at night. Then he went to a private chat room and would minimize the screen as I would walk into the room. One time the phone rang at one-thirty A.M. in the morning. It was the first time I knew something was amiss. I started to catch on there was a woman calling my house when he forgot to erase the caller ID and I saw it was a California number (we are in Michigan). I got a program to catch the passwords and to bring back deleted e-mail. They said they were in love with each other and had never felt so bonded spiritually and emotionally. I called up AT&T and got the name of the person. It turned out it wasn't Tina, but Angela, and upon further checking the woman was a Catholic (and female) version of David Koresh. Nothing she said checked out. I confronted my husband about what was going on and told his family, but they live in denial and don't believe what he did. We're now divorced as I invaded his personal space by taping the phone calls. I did stop him from seeing the woman at first by confronting him about their meeting plans. I have gotten copies of his long distance bills and he calls her eight to twelve times a day, any hour of the day or night. Please don't use my name. Oh, yes . . . she now is Director of Religious Education at a Catholic Church—what a hypocrite.

The second way the Internet can impact a marriage comes from the development of relationships online, even with no one intending to do so. I believe there are a large number of people who accidentally meet someone online and develop an intense relationship while spending time online. This relationship can be exclusively online or it may (as it often does) leave the Net to find itself as a real-time affair. There are many variations to this process, but they all involve spending large amounts of time online. As a result there is less time spent on their primary relationship. All good relationships require time to be spent together, and if that time is spent online chatting or having cybersex than there has to be less time and energy left for real-time living.

The power of crossing the line online is further amplified by the fact that online relationships often feel so intimate to both participants. In our study we found that over 40 percent of people online felt the Internet was a way to experience intimacy. For Internet addicts, that figure jumped to 75 percent! As I previously stated, this intimacy can seem so powerful that normal relationships pale by comparison. It's hard to contrast a new and exciting cyber-romance, complete with great cyber-sex, with the more earthy realities of staring at your spouse of twenty years across the breakfast table! In general this is true—it's hard for your real-life experiences to compete with the expansiveness of the cyberworld. The Net provides a sense of "freeness" and "openness" to communication, and this accelerated intimacy develops to the point that one can become virtually swept away in a new relationship without even realizing it.

How to Tell If Your Loved One Is a Nethead

Here are thirteen Internet addiction warning signs to look for. What you're assessing is your loved one's overall pattern of behavior, usually for a period of at least three to six months. If you see a few of these signs in your loved one, then it might be worth talking to them, or better yet give them a copy of this book to read. Help them come to some awareness on their own. The readiness for change has many stages and sometimes all you can do is help provide the seeds of information to initiate the process of change.

People must change at their own pace as there are stages in preparing to change. This usually begins as *thinking* about changing, then progressing to *preparing* to change, finally moving on to *action* and then *maintenance* (Prochaska and DiClemente 1986).

Thirteen Warning Signs of Internet Addiction in Your Spouse, Friend, or Loved One

Recognizing the warning signs of Internet addiction in your spouse or loved one is the first step in your helping them help themselves. The following warning signs should serve as general guidelines for you to determine whether or not your spouse, family member, or friend may have a problem. Does your loved one:

1. Spend a lot of time alone with their computer on a regular basis?

2. Become defensive when you confront them with their behavior.

3. Seem either unaware of what they have been doing, or attempt to deny it.

4. Prefer spending time with their computer or on the Internet than with you or other people.

5. Lose interest in other, previously important activities, e.g., friends, sports, work, hobbies, exercise, etc.

6. Appear to be more socially isolated, moody, or irritable.

7. Seem to be establishing "a second life," with new and different friends whom they met online.

8. Spend greater amounts of time online, and attempt to cover or "minimize" the screen when you come in the room.

9. Arrange unexpected time away from home on business trips or for other reasons, and seem to be away more than usual (this can be for out-of-town liaisons to meet up with cyberlovers)

10. Have unexplained charges on your credit card bill, and offer suspicious explanations.

11. Exhibit signs that their work or school performance is suffering, e.g., they were fired, grades are slipping, or their household responsibilities are neglected.

12. Talk about their time on the computer incessantly, and seem to draw meaning in their life from this activity.

13. Have legal problems as a result of their Internet behavior, e.g., loss of child custody, divorce, or sexual harassment charges at work due to downloading pornography, etc.

If these warning signs sound similar to the signs of having an affair, that's because they are. Internet addiction is a lot like having an affair, an affair with a computer, along with their relationships formed online. It's the same process whenever a person withdraws from their main source of support (spouse, friends, family) and finds it elsewhere (in this case on the Internet).

Cyberspace Intervention

There have always been threats to marriages and relationships. Even without external pressures, keeping a marriage or relationship alive and well is no easy task. Good marriages require ongoing work. They need constant attention, just as a garden requires daily care. The longer you let your gardening go, the more difficult the work becomes. If you let a garden go for a few weeks, it dies. Fortunately, primary relationships are a bit more resilient than gardens, but they too have their breaking point. Often, the slow erosion of this relationship goes unnoticed until it's too late. I cannot tell you how many times I've had a husband sitting in my office telling me he had no idea things were this bad; this is *after* his wife has indicated that she'd been telling him for years! Good marriages are hard, bad ones are harder, but they are initially easy because there is usually little energy being expended in a productive direction.

What Makes the Net So Sexy?

The Internet poses just one more external threat. One more time drain and distraction for your attention. Add this to the myriad of tasks that already bombards us every day: TV, radio, fax, telephone, e-mail, voice mail, pagers, cell phones, and so on. Television alone, in my opinion, creates significant problems in marriages and relationships today. *It's easier to watch TV than to talk.* Unfortunately, conversation is the only reliable method to enhance intimacy, and the type of conversation I'm advocating can't be done between commercials. To further complicate matters, children, money, sex, jobs, friends, cars, hobbies, religion, house, and school all require time and energy, making intimate time more difficult to find. The Net can streamline and digitize intimacy to fit into your busy life!

So what's so sexy about the Internet? After all, isn't it just another invention that grabs our attention? In some ways yes, but this is the first invention that is truly *interactive*, and it is this interactivity that creates the powerful attraction that ultimately threatens your marriage or relationship. The interactivity allows one to truly connect with the communication experience. Unlike TV or the telephone, where there is an almost flat, two-dimensional quality, the Internet is vibrant and alive. It is dynamic, just as relationships can be. In order to snap out of your Internet infatuation, you need to take steps to enhance the intensity of your *real-time living*.

Ten Steps to Reclaim Your Marriage or Relationship

Step 1. *Make your marriage or relationship the priority in your life.* Most people put their relationship at the bottom of the pile to be attended to with leftover time. But there's never "extra" time, thus the relationship never gets the attention it needs. Most couples, with or without Internet problems, make their relationship such a low priority that their emotional needs often do not get met. There are a great many things that can get in the way of focusing on your couplehood first, most typically children. What many parents/ spouses do not realize is that being a good parent starts with being a good partner. If you don't recognize your relationship as a significant part of your life, it will *cease being part of your life*. No tree can survive without good strong roots and remember that a relationship is a *process*, not an *outcome*, it requires ongoing maintenance and attention.

Step 2. *Set up boundaries for how much time you or your significant other will spend online.* Limit your time to the most necessary uses. Create a clear agreement as to what is reasonable for each of you. These boundaries also apply to other areas of your life that may be encroaching on your precious time together. *Be clear and specific about what you will be changing.* If you use e-mail a lot, try snail mail or faxing, or consider that truly retro-device, the telephone! If you or your loved one is addicted to the Net, access to the computer must be limited and the limitations adhered to.

Step 3. *Cut off contact with romantic cyberfriends.* Do not engage in cybersex, phonesex, cybering, chat room visits, or visitation to adult Web sites.

Step 4. *Reduce your television viewing time.* There is often a correlation between TV viewing and relationship problems and there is preliminary support of this in our research. Television is a distraction from productive communication. In addition, TV viewing can act as a trigger for continued Internet use as there is a psychological overlap between the two.

Step 5. *Set aside time alone with each other on a regular basis.* This time has to be protected and treated with utmost respect. If each of you sees the other doing this, it conveys how important the relationship is to each other. This can start the process toward healing the relationship and create a positive feeling about your commitment to one another. It is critical that the time is protected from all the encroachments of life—resist the temptation to put it off until next week. Sometimes next week never comes.

Step 6. *Work on communicating more effectively.* Take time to focus on the part of your marriage that is still healthy. At the same time, address the impact of your loved one's Internet addiction on your relationship. Be honest, open, and willing to take emotional risks. You have to give up the importance of "being right," because if you're right, then someone is wrong. If someone is wrong, then they feel bad. If they feel badly, you've won the battle but lost the war. You've gained nothing.

Step 7. *Obtain counseling or psychotherapy with someone with qualified experience in addictions treatment.* Find a therapist with experience in Internet addiction. You may have trouble finding someone with direct Internet addiction experience, but try to find someone who is at least open to the idea. Above all, find someone with whom you're both comfortable. The psychologist may wish to have both husband and wife present for the visits, which can be very helpful.

Step 8. *Spend some extended time alone together.* Travel if you can. Try to get away for weekend trips (or even just overnight). The idea is to spend time alone doing new, exciting, and fun things. This will help substitute some of the excitement and fun that was derived from the Internet. It is especially important that you spend time together focused on the affectionate and emotional aspects of your marriage or relationship, which will help renew the emotional reserves needed to sustain you through tough times.

Step 9. *Introduce new romantic and sexual activities.* Try to add new spice to your love life. Share a sexy novel, give each other messages, try some sexy lingerie, and share your innermost fantasies with each other, just as you might with someone online. You might even try writing your loved one a love letter, since you've gotten comfortable sharing your sentiments in writing on the Net.

Step 10. *Consider a support group.* There are numerous support groups for Internet addicts. Many of these support groups have sections available for spouses and loved ones as well. Unfortunately, many of the support groups meet online, which makes them of less use to someone who is addicted to the Internet. *Cyberwidows* is a support group for spouses of Internet addicts and has valuable information for those frustrated with sharing their husband or wife with a computer. (There are also other resources listed in the Resources section in the back of this book.)

Give Your Relationship an Intimacy Tune-up

Give your relationship an intimacy tune-up. The following are some general guidelines I developed for my practice for all couples who need to recharge their marital and relational batteries. The suggestions include methods and techniques that a couple can use to improve their personal interactions. These serve only as suggestions and may not apply to all couples or situations, but they can be beneficial.

- Try to recognize and acknowledge the feelings and thoughts of each other. Let your significant other know that you understand what they're saying. To do this, repeat or paraphrase what you've heard; do not interpret, deny, or change what you heard them say. Simply say it back so they know you understand. Do not try to solve their problem; just acknowledge that you heard them.
- When communicating your negative feelings, try to discuss the behavior that upset you. Do not bring up old stuff, past experiences, or a general assessment of their personality or character. Be specific and avoid generalizations.
- Do something pleasing for each other on a regular basis. A way to do this is for both partners to make lists of things they enjoy, and write these activities on slips of paper, then put the slips into jars—one for each of you. When you feel like doing something nice for your partner, reach in the jar and pull out a slip. Then do it—right away, so you don't forget. Remember that there will always be reasons to not do something nice for your partner. Try to do it anyway, even if "they don't deserve it" or "they haven't done anything for me first." You're investing in creating a "quality relationship" (Jacobson and Margolin 1979).

- Remember that both partners contribute to relationship problems. Arguments, fights, disagreements, and unhappiness tend to be mutually caused and maintained. No one is singly responsible. When a couple can openly acknowledge their mutual contribution to problems, they're well on their way to solving them.
- Take time alone, away from the children and work commitments on a regular basis. Often couples forget that their relationship needs nurturing and attention separate from children, jobs, and household responsibilities. It's important to reinforce the romance and friendship in a marriage on a regular basis. Marriages and relationships cannot grow without attention and focus.
- Recognize that marriage and relationships change over time, and that the changes need not be negative. Romantic love isn't the only form of loving. The intimate friendship that can grow from romance can, in the long run, be even more rewarding than the excitement and newness of romantic love. Romance never fades completely; it simply changes over time, and ebbs and flows.
- Try to develop friendships and interests outside of the relationship. Bring your new interests and ideas to share with your loved one. Your relationship can only be as interesting as each of you are to yourselves. A relationship is made up of what you each bring into it, and the more you give to each other, the more you'll get back.
- Though you may sometimes feel that you "give" too much, or give more than your partner, you are investing in a relationship that you intend to last. It will balance out in the long run. Temporary sacrifices will result in long-term gains.
- Be aware that, over time, things you found most likable about each other may fade. This is normal; the longer you're together, the more you get used to each

other. New ideas, experiences, and behaviors are necessary to keep you interested in each other. Often things you found attractive can become annoying—examine those parts of yourself that you may not like and see if your partner is reminding you of them.

- Marriage is an ongoing process that requires attention, effort, and compromise. As you grow and change as individuals, so too must the relationship change. The marriage ceremony is the beginning of a work-in-progress.

- When a conflict arises, be prepared to problem-solve and brainstorm some ideas to resolve the problem. Don't expect 100 percent satisfaction; you're dealing with the needs of another person, as well as your own. If you're both willing to give an inch, there will be far more room to strike a balance between each of your needs.

- Remember the goal of fighting is to resolve conflict, not to win a "battle." Winners have to have losers, and winners ultimately "stand alone." You can agree to disagree and take a break from your conflict. If it's important, it will be there when you get back.

- Try to remember that your goal is to grow individually while also enhancing your partner's "Self." Uplifting your partner will ultimately expand you, as well.

Rescuing your relationship from cyberspace requires the same skills needed to face any challenge to your relationship. Recommit your attention and energy to focusing on the relationship, and begin to do something different than before. Simply making a commitment to spend more time together can make a huge difference. The point is to change some of the basic patterns that may be contributing to being stuck in the relationship. Remember that Internet addiction is a reminder that work has to be done on your marriage or relationship!

8

The E-Store

*Shopping and Investing
the World Online*

Convenience is the mother of invention.

If there ever was any doubt as to whether or not Internet shopping would take off, there no longer is. The 1998 Christmas season demonstrated that e-commerce is growing into a sizable way we do our shopping. Santa often came into our home this year through a modem instead of the chimney. Sites like *E-Bay, Amazon.com, E-Toys, Macy's.com, Lands End, EggHead.com,* and of course Dell, experienced the joys of the electronic Christmas season rush. People are no longer spending their hard-earned e-dollars only on adult Web sites.

The Internet has gone mainstream, in a big way. And this trend continues to grow. There were approximately $10 billion spent online in 1998, with estimates of future exponential growth, perhaps reflecting up to 10 percent of United States retail sales in the very near future. This number may be even higher when the Internet becomes better linked to our TVs and it has the memory capacity to store relevant financial information. Eventually, all you may need to do is a high-speed surf to your favorite e-store and with one push of a button order what you want. All the personal data, including credit card and shipping information, will already be stored as a default, so it will be like ordering a pay-per-view movie: instant access and order processing. Many of the larger *e-tail* (electronic retail) sites are moving toward larger product lines or joint ventures, linking up with other sites that complement their product lines. And the goal is always the same—offer a selection, at a good price, and make the transaction as easy as possible.

In our research, we found that 58 percent of the Net users we surveyed made purchases online. That number is probably increasing as you read this book! There are estimates that the Internet may become the preferred modality of making purchases for certain products and services, including airline, bus, and rail services; electronics; collectibles; automobile information and sales; auction sales; book, tape, and software sales; financial and investment services; and last but not least, sexually-related materials. One major airline recently announced that it would charge a $2 premium for tickets *not* purchased online. It seems likely that, whatever the numbers, the Internet will be a strong force in commerce, with some estimates totaling even higher than the 10 percent of United States retail sales that I noted earlier.

The Internet: A Compulsive Shopper's Dream, or Nightmare?

People can become addicted to shopping as they would any other drug or behavior. Most of us have experienced the pleasant sensation we get after buying something. Unfortunately, that feeling is short-lived, and may be followed by a sense of guilt or remorse, perhaps leading us to return the item. It even has a name: *buyer's remorse.* Yet we often repeat this pattern of buying and feeling remorseful, in spite of the negative feelings it may bring. The repetition of this pattern indicates how powerful good feelings are in motivating us, and how quickly we forget the pain or discomfort this process may cause.

Consumer Bulimia

I call this pattern *consumer bulimia,* named after the difficult eating disorder where you binge on food and then vomit it up out of guilt, because the process is similar. We like the feeling of buying something new. It's fun to have a new toy, but it may only serve as a temporary distraction from the more mundane aspects of our daily lives. Shopping can be used as an anesthetic. Like any drug, it temporarily numbs us from our feelings and takes our mind off bigger (and harder) issues in our lives.

This doesn't mean that everyone who shops a lot is a shopaholic, or that if they use the Internet for shopping, they'll become hopelessly addicted to surfing for bargains. Patients do tell me, however, that they find themselves getting hooked on auction sites like *E-Bay* and *Priceline.com,* perpetually searching for bargains. E-Bay and Priceline.com are virtual stores where goods, products, and services are bid on and sold to the highest bidder. E-Bay typically deals with used, as opposed to new merchandise. I recently did an interview on the topic of Web auction addiction, where people discussed creating an almost compulsive computer-based hobby. This is the case for many people because having the Net at your disposal for shopping offers you literally infinite opportunities in the form of choice, price, and e-tailer. And, it's the promise of the illusive *best deal* that seems to propel us toward compulsive use or abuse of e-commerce. Online, the quantity of choices available, along with the twenty-four-hour availability, and potentially lower prices, creates a unique, but potentially addictive, consumer experience in cyberspace.

It's Too Easy!

The fact that it is so easy to shop online makes e-shopping quite addictive. You only need a credit card (and sometimes that's even unnecessary) and access to a computer to have all the world's products and services at your fingertips. Surfing e-stores on the Web is a lot like browsing or window shopping in a traditional store, but much easier. Owning a computer is even becoming unnecessary as Web TV has begun to grow, and eventually I believe that the TV will be the central portal to the Web in our homes. Shopping online is fast. You can browse and shop all day and enjoy the spoils by overnight mail tomorrow. Talk about instant gratification! You don't even have to leave the comfort of your home or office as you cover the equivalent of a mall (and that mall could even be in, say, Paris!), without getting sore feet! Even with sore fingers, there's no doubt that it's more convenient to shop online once you've mastered the Web.

Online shopping is probably so addictive because it uses the Internet (which is itself addictive) *and* you're getting a "hit" from making an Internet purchase. So not only are you experiencing the Internet adventure, where you don't know exactly what you're going to find next, but you're also getting a false sense of filling up an emotional void with your purchase. Every new page and hyperlink becomes a gateway to an unknown jackpot, and this can be exciting. Internet addicts may therefore be much more likely than nonaddicted Internet users to become compulsive online shoppers. Again, this is because of the excessive use, disinhibition, ease of access, and availability the Internet brings. In our research we found that about 4 percent of nonaddicted Internet users reported being addicted to any type of shopping, while 14 percent of those addicted to the Net reported being addicted to shopping of all kinds as well.

How Safe in Cyberspace: The Perils of Purchasing Online

How safe is it to buy things online? Well, one Web based e-commerce site that is gaining a lot of attention is *E-Bay*. They auction off privately owned merchandise. It acts as a broker, and for a small fee, it will connect interested buyers to sellers. There does have to be trust in the whole system to warrant sending your money off to a stranger and hoping to receive your purchase. With E-Bay, for example, you're buying from private individuals, where you don't have the protection of using a credit card to make your purchases. Most of the time it works. Sometimes it doesn't. There are many new auction-based sites appearing, reflecting the popularity of making purchases this way in spite of the potential risks.

There are also many e-commerce sites that operate more like traditional mail-order catalogs, selling their products on Web pages instead of paper ones. Most major retailers now have online e-stores operating and with steadily growing sales. We have come to a point in the development of the Web where a retailer can no longer afford *not* to have a presence online.

Pay with Plastic

The best rule of thumb is to *always use your credit card* when purchasing on the Internet, unless you're buying from an auction site like E-Bay, where you're dealing with private individuals and must use cash or a check. Sometimes a money order or bank check may be required by some auction site sellers.

Fortunately, using your credit card online gives you the same legal redress as traditional stores if things don't look as good in real-time as they did online. A recent article in *Time* Magazine (Krantz 1998) discussed the benefits of using credit cards for online purchases. This caution may not be as necessary with well-established retailers who would likely honor their return policy, but is *essential* if you're unfamiliar with those you're buying from.

I, for example, had an experience with a computer parts company from whom I ordered a new hard drive. I couldn't get the part to work, so I called to arrange for a refund, which they authorized. I sent the item back, but I never received a refund, nor did I get the item back! Since this occurred I haven't been able to reach them by phone and they appear to have gone out of business. This brings up another problem with virtual shopping: you don't have any physical proof of the company's existence other than their Web page, which anyone can easily produce! Luckily I paid with a VISA card and I am dealing with it through VISA, who will guarantee my payment. Had I used a check or cash or one of the new Web currencies I'd be out of luck.

The Internet is likely to continue to reshape the manner in which we buy and sell our wares, and as the ease and safety of shopping online continues to develop, more of us will turn to the Web to do our shopping. Just as there was an explosion in compulsive shopping that occurred when TV shopping channels started, the Internet is undoubtedly spawning a new breed of Internet shopping addicts.

Pros and Cons of Shopping in Cyberland

The Pros:

- The Internet offers extreme convenience and is the ultimate "shop-at-home-in-your PJs" experience.
- You always have access to the latest merchandise, along with the most recent changes in model or specifications. You also have good access to excess inventory, discontinued items, and overruns.
- You don't have to spend money on gas, tolls, or parking, or get stuck in traffic when using your car or other transportation.

- You can save a lot of time.
- You will often save on sales tax because you're purchasing online, and taking delivery through the mail. (Be sure to check with your state office of revenue or taxation for the specifics.)
- You have an infinitely wide selection.
- You can often find lower prices online.
- You won't have to waste time looking at products that are too high or low for your budget, as a lot of retailers tailor their ads and promotions to your specific interests or buying patterns. They may only send you information about products and services that are specifically suited to your interests, education, and financial status. This information will be based on previous shopping patterns.
- You will *only* see what is most likely to appeal to you. This "GoldieLocks" (just right) type of marketing can be so fine-tuned that it will save the e-store on advertising costs, which can be later passed on to you.
- You enjoy some degree of anonymity online with your purchases and can shop in secret!

The Cons:

- You never know what you're going to get and sometimes what you see *isn't* what you get!
- The Net still has the potential for fraud and unproven companies, and the lack of a storefront creates a consumer blind spot.
- Online shopping can become habitual and financially risky and you may find yourself becoming addicted. This can often be seen when purchasing stocks and investments from online brokers. You can now buy stocks or bonds online instantly, and the industry has seen near-exponential growth. The problem is that many people are buying too impulsively due to the ease of doing so, along with the easy availability of margin purchasing.

- You don't have the fun and social experience of being with people while you shop (this can actually be a con at Christmas).
- Sometimes the prices aren't lower, and may actually be higher.
- You can lose some of your anonymity online, as they will track your Web purchases via "cookies," and e-mail capture for targeted marketing purposes.
- Online shopping can distort your awareness of the money you spend and you may find yourself spending money more easily than you'd like to.
- Selections may be limited on the merchants Web page, as compared to shopping in their store or by mail-order catalog.

No Shangri-La

Shopping online can be an exciting and cost-saving experience, but can also be fraught with problems. For example, Laurie loved the new laptop computer she brought home from the office. Her boss suggested she take it home to get familiar with how it works and to spend some time on the Internet. Laurie, who described herself as a "technophobe," didn't even know how to get onto the Internet, nor did she really know what the Internet was.

One Friday night, however, Laurie brought her laptop home, determined to try to get on to the Internet. After what seemed like hours, she finally got online and was amazed as she entered the world of the Internet! The colors, sounds, and flash astounded her. It reminded her of TV, but also felt like she was on the strip of Las Vegas! Laurie remembers the initial excitement, and spending four hours online that first night. She figured it was because it was a novelty and that it would wear off. But the next night she found herself online again for another five hours!

Just as the newness began to wear off after a week or so, Laurie discovered some of her favorite stores had Web sites.

Now she was really having fun! She found that she could surf for all the merchandise she wanted in a fraction of the time it would take her to shop on foot. She soon discovered all the specials that could only be found online. Laurie was thrilled. The first night alone she spent over two thousand dollars in just under two hours! Laurie was so excited—she felt exhilarated, almost high. This process went on for about a month. She bought a new wardrobe, a new computer of her own, a camera, some new dishes, an oriental rug, and she even began her Christmas shopping for that year, even though it was only July!

After a month or so Laurie got her first credit card bill. She was shocked when she saw a fifteen thousand dollar balance. She swore to return as many items as she could, but it turned out she had used most of them, and had thrown away the shipping containers. Her initial excitement turned to frustration as she realized she was going into tremendous debt. In spite of all this, Laurie was online nearly every night looking for more bargains. It was too hard to resist! She was even beginning to use the auction sites to look for bargains on things she didn't really need.

Laurie continued to buys things because it "felt" good, and she got a "hit" after each purchase, and again after she received the package. This "high" was soon followed by an overwhelming sense of guilt and remorse, which she dealt with by escaping and going online and shopping some more. She tried to stop, but couldn't. Her Internet shopping became a daily routine. Finally, after she received her second credit card bill for another twelve thousand dollars, Laurie had to admit to herself that she was addicted, and that she needed help!

Admitting her problem to herself freed her to begin to look at her behavior and to get help. First, she joined an overspenders support group. Then she arranged for individual counseling so that she could get control of her life. Her therapist helped Laurie to develop a plan to deal with the potential for relapse, and she began to examine some of the emptiness in her life that led to her addiction in the first place. Laurie also hired a debt consolidation service to assist her in paying off the twenty thousand dollar debts she'd built up in just two months! After six months Laurie was on her way back to real-time sanity. She decided to cancel her online service, and to follow the strict budget she was placed on by the debt counselor. She also decided that when she had to shop, she'd just have to do it the old-fashioned, low-tech way!

Can You Become an Online Shopping Addict?

The answer is yes. Most people who use computers are generally of at least average intelligence. You might then be asking how you could possibly become addicted to online shopping? But think back to chapter 2 when we discussed how you can become addicted to behaviors because of changes in brain chemistry. Interacting with two powerful mood-enhancers like the Internet and shopping creates a formidable experience for those of us who may be prone to becoming addicted to either.

Shopping and the Internet make a perfect combination. Unlike TV, the interactive nature of online shopping and buying creates a very personal shopping experience. And remember, eventually the ads, e-mails, and banners sent to you will be targeted specifically to your interests and tastes, based on your previous purchases. These are designed to maximize the likelihood of your making a purchase.

You may find yourself logging on to the Net one day and finding a personalized invitation to a fashion show displaying clothing styles you typically order displayed in your size and color preference! There are already virtual coupons and online-only sales that enhance the value of Web shopping and create another addictive thrill: a great bargain. These new digital marketing techniques are there to encourage you to do as much shopping as possible online.

As the Net becomes more integrated into our daily lives, it's becoming harder to avoid the triggers that might cause us to experience a relapse from a destructive Internet pattern such as compulsive shopping. Compulsive e-shopping can also create the experience of tolerance and withdrawal where you need to buy greater quantities or higher values of what you purchase followed by a potential psychological withdrawal when you break the addictive pattern.

The Net Was Made to Sell

The Internet is a perfect medium for selling. This makes you an even more likely candidate for compulsive shopping. Besides the potential for targeted sales, choice, convenience, and speed, the virtual store can keep their expenses lower due to less overhead when compared to their brick-and-mortar counterparts. Perhaps the best-known example of online retailing is *Amazon.com*. They became the world's largest online retailer of books, tapes, and videos, virtually overnight. Although the profits are still long in coming, the sales figures reflect a concept that clearly works, and is continuing to grow. Even companies such as *EggHead.com* (formally EggHead Software) decided to close their retail stores and do business exclusively on the Net.

There are countless examples of companies that have either added Internet sales, or continue to expand them. There are also those companies that have created niche industries online, and are poised to be the "category killers of the Web." While working on this book, I met someone who'd just opened a health insurance company that exclusively used the Net for sales and was totally Web based. Many industries are likely to find that the Web may become the most suitable method to sell their products or services.

I predict that we are headed for such personalized and focused sales campaigns from retailers that it will make traditional junk mail almost obsolete. The marketing you'll receive will be more relevant, and may even be timed to coincide with your needs, such as your kids' birthdays, or your anniversary! You will receive invitations to buy products and services that they not only know you'll like, but through previous sales records, they'll know exactly what you'll need and when. Add this personalized selling to an instant Web credit line, the ability to buy from any location, and you have a click-and-buy society. The problem is, it's so easy to browse, buy, and order online, that it makes compulsive and addictive shopping a virtual trap. It is like putting a bar on every corner in a neighborhood of alcoholics, or even worse, putting the bar in front of your job, where you have to pass it every day. Great care and self-control must be taken to limit your access to online shopping and to recognize when you're beginning to "click" a little too frequently.

Taking Stock of the Market

Another area of growing sales is in the area of *stock* and *bond trades*. Those of you who follow the stock market may have heard how well the Internet brokerages are doing. Many of them are less than two years old and are beginning to rival some of the better-established traditional brokerage houses. Even traditional brokerage houses that previously shunned the Web have seen the "digital light" and are now going online. However, the relative ease of online stock trading makes buying stocks seem less real. And when you add the ability to buy on margin, you're increasing the risks associated with this form of virtual gambling. (Buying stocks on margin essentially means you are borrowing money from your broker to buy stocks or bonds. It's a loan, complete with interest.) There are two dangers to buying on margin that are elevated by Web investing. The first is that, because you are not dealing with a person, there is no feedback. It is too easy to point and click in an impulsive way. A recent issue of *Barron's* reported record levels of margin buying, which it attributes to Web investors. The second danger is that so may stocks purchased are high tech/Internet related and are therefore very volatile. If the values of your stocks drop below a certain point, there can be what is called a "margin call" where you have to put more cash into your account or risk having your stocks sold—this is because the stocks you own act as collateral for your margin loan, so as your collateral drops in value (when the market drops) you have less available collateral and need to put more cash in to guarantee your loan. Some financial experts regard margin purchasing of high-risk stocks to be more like gambling than investing. Buying on margin can give it that extra "kick" from the risk, which can have devastating financial consequences if not done reasonably. That doesn't mean that Web investing is inherently dangerous. It isn't. For most people it works quite well, while for others the combination of the Internet, poor investing habits, as well as margin purchasing can be problematic.

Losing Touch with Real-Time Investing

Stock investing is a form of gambling. That is, it is not a sure thing, as no investment can be, but the risk increases when combining stock investing with the Internet. Just like online shopping, stock investing online loses some of the markers that make it realistic, such as:

- Calling a broker
- Writing a check
- Researching the stock
- Talking it over with your spouse
- Taking your time to think your investment through

Click a few times and in one minute you can own a stock without really taking the time to research or track it. This may not be a problem for most people, but for someone who is either addicted to the Internet or is into high-risk investing (gambling), it can be a destructive combination. For such people, online investing can be too easy and therefore too tempting. In fact, many of the Internet brokerages have instituted policies on margin purchases online, especially with regard to high-risk and speculative stocks, which are often Internet-related companies with little or no earnings history! This may be even more critical for options or commodities investing, where the volatility is so high.

Charles Schwab reports that in 1998 fifty-eight percent of *all* the stock trades they processed were online trades! Only two short years ago that number was essentially zero! Again, there is no denying the power and convenience of the Internet, and it's that very powerful ease of access that makes purchasing *anything* online so tempting. I fear that once the Net becomes more accessible through faster and cheaper connections, there will be a deluge of inexperienced investors and shoppers, which can lead to a potentially compulsive experience. For some, an addiction may follow, necessitating some form of help.

What Can You Do?

The first step in changing any pattern is to *recognize the problem,* or begin to recognize the potential for a problem to occur. First, ask yourself the following questions to see if you've been letting "your fingers do the walking" on the keyboard too often.

- You've been spending too much money online.
- You're buying things you don't really need online.
- You find yourself checking the sale pages on your favorite e-stores regularly.
- You've been book-marking every shopping site you can find.
- You've run up a large credit card balance.
- You're friends or family have expressed concern about your Web shopping or investing.
- You're keeping the amount of time and money you spend online a secret.
- You're experiencing frequent cycles of purchasing or investing, followed by guilt, shame, or remorse (and possibly trying to return or sell the items), only to repeat the pattern again.

- You're having significant financial problems, such as margin calls, bankruptcy, liens, foreclosures, repossessions, evictions, or utility shut-offs.
- You're having marital or relationship problems as a result of your compulsive Internet shopping or investing pattern.
- You're having legal problems as a result of e-shopping or Web investing.

If you answer "yes" to five or more, you may have a problem with your compulsive shopping or investing online.

Twelve Techniques for the Compulsive Cybershopper and Investor

1. Turn off the computer after each time you use it. Having to boot up and log on each time can act as a deterrent to going online and shopping or investing.

2. Decide on what (if anything) you need before going online to shop, write it down on a piece of paper, and when you do decide, make *only* that one purchase.

3. Try not going to a site and browsing the products or stocks; this may be too tempting for some people.

4. If you want to make a purchase, consider ordering by mail or telephone. This may help decrease some of the Internet disinhibition that can give way to compulsive spending online.

5. Try not to shop online alone. If you have to go online, do so only with a friend or family member, and be sure to tell them that you may have a problem with compulsive Internet shopping so they'll be able to support your limit setting.

6. Don't keep your problem a secret. Talk to others about it and enlist their active support. The more secrecy, the

greater the potential for shame, which can lead to further compulsive shopping as a means to deal with negative feelings. This cycle can become a repetitive pattern if not addressed.

7. Do all your investing through the telephone or a live broker. The ease and isolation of online investing can be very risky for those addicted to the Internet or for those addicted to stock investing, which may itself be a form of compulsive gambling.

8. Stop and think before logging on. When you want to purchase something, think about whether *you really* need the item(s) you're about to buy. Ask yourself if it is important

   to have the item or whether you can live without it. After all, you have been living without it for so long.

9. Do not spend more time than is necessary using a computer or the Internet. The less time you spend online, the less likely you are to browse and order items.

10. Limit your access to credit cards when you're online. Follow a budget for any new purchases. Tear up your credit cards if you have to.

11. Consider seeking financial or psychological counseling to assist you in dealing with compulsive online shopping.

12. Join debtors anonymous, gamblers ananymous, or an overspenders support group.

It is difficult to fight the attraction of low prices, great selection, easy access, and twenty-four hour availability of the Internet. Add this to the multimedia fun of the Internet and you have the *Home Shopping Network* on steroids! It seems clear that the combination of the Internet and shopping are a lot like peanut butter and jelly, very sticky, but they go well together. It's necessary to maintain vigilance when addressing this new and potent combination and the world of buying online.

9

The Web at Work

On the Net Instead of on the Job

Technology is of no advantage if it doesn't improve the quality of our daily lives.

Technology has undoubtedly improved the quality of our lives at work. The Web has even further opened up new avenues for increased productivity, greater flexibility, and new applications for the work we do. We now have the ability to instantly access a virtually unlimited fountain of information in the corporate environment. This has opened up many new horizons for most businesses, and in doing so is creating a global integration of the world's information economy. Not only do most businesses have instant access to any information they may want or need, but they can also use the Internet to integrate all of their office locations, or make more information available locally.

Our research indicates that approximately *29 percent of time spent online is done while at work.* This figure seems to be slightly higher (33 percent) for Internet addicts. This fact is not lost on entrepreneurs who make software called "boss screens" that allow you to toggle back and forth between what you're surfing for and a *fake desktop screen*! This method would allow you to *look busy* when you are in fact *not working*! Although most businesses probably expect some degree of personal use of the Internet from their employees (just as they do for the telephone and the copier), they're probably not prepared for the *three hours* or so a day that Internet addicts are spending online at work. This means that, for an Internet addict, *over one-third* of the workday is spent online! The financial costs of this cyberdiversion are probably seen in the form of reduced productivity and decrease in efficiency. These financial losses have prompted new companies to create Web monitoring software that track all Web traffic in and out of each desktop or terminal!

The Internet's Place In the Business World

A *server* is actually a computer with a large hard drive memory capacity. It's usually the center of a LAN (local area network) where each desk-top computer connects with the server, which stores information for everyone to access. The ability to utilize the *Internet* as the company's server is beginning to take hold. Businesses like Sun Microsystems and Oracle have talked about this possibility for years. Not only will the Net serve as an information repository, but it might eventually serve the function that a mainframe computer or a network server does presently. All software applications and data will be held in secure servers at some remote location with multiple backup protections. This would allow for a more efficient storage and

retrieval of software and data because a business could theoretically share software with other users, while maintaining
separate secure data.

This system would be more cost efficient by avoiding
duplicative applications (and hardware), as well as the efficiency of making information accessible to *appropriate users* in
the company. Because of the Internet's universal accessibility
from anywhere in the world, employees working from home
offices will be able to have access to any applications and data
they need, from wherever they are. We will soon begin to the
see the advent of the global office!

The Internet is at the cutting edge of an expanded usefulness on the job. Most employers see the potential uses of the
Internet, and have begun to make the Net available to worksta-
tions and computers on the job. And after all, why not? The
Net is being hailed as the greatest technological advance since
the telephone or TV, exceeding both in growth rates and
acceptance. You cannot go a day without hearing about the
newest Internet technology or application. Each week brings a
new IPO to the stock market, furthering the "gold-rush men-
tality" of the Internet. No one wants to be left behind on this
technological rocket, in part because of potential financial
gains. Just as in the gold rush of the 1800s, there may be some
casualties along the way, and Internet abuse and addiction
may be one such casualty.

Netheads at Work

With all this growth and promise, what could be the
problem? Well, there is ample evidence that many employees
are abusing the Internet while on the job. For Internet addicts
who have access at work, our research suggests that upwards
of *three hours a day* may be spent online at work. The problem
is not new, but it's probably growing as more companies make
fast Internet service available on the job. The problem may not
be so serious yet that the business community feels they need
to deal with it. After all, Internet abuse and addiction are

somewhat secretive; no one really knows what employees are doing online (although some employers are beginning to monitor Web access). I have no doubt that employees are using the Internet for personal use on the job. The extent of this abuse still remains to be seen.

I am personally aware of numerous cases of employees who have described the significant time they wasted online instead of doing their work. They would spend upwards of three to four hours of the workday cybersurfing. This translates into a significant economic loss for their employer. And most of the employees with a problem aren't even aware of the fact that they're addicted, until after they're fired for violating company policy or poor work performance.

"Violating company policy" may refer to cases in which people have been fired for exposing their co-workers to sexually explicit material. Many companies have strict rules regarding the downloading of pornographic material, and in many cases this violates the sexual harassment policies adhered to by most businesses. I've heard of more job terminations due to downloading pornography than any other Internet-related cause!

Take John's story. John was a successful executive in a large insurance company who loved the Internet. He particularly liked adult Web sites, so much so that he started his day by closing his office door, pouring a cup of coffee, and logging on to the company's high-speed Internet connection. From there, he would surf the myriad of pornography sites, sometimes spending two-thirds of his ten-hour workday online! John would usually find a particular Web site that appealed to him and download its X-rated contents to his hard drive.

One day, John had just finished downloading and saving a new crop of choice photos when he was informed that the MIS technician was scheduled to service his PC at noon. John had no time to delete the thousands of photos on his eight gig hard drive. The technician found the saved porn, and John was reported to Human Resources for violating the company's Internet use policy. John was fired the next day. This story highlights the power and problems with easy access to very addictive information. John is not alone, and I have little doubt that businesses are losing millions of dollars through wasted productivity.

The Lowdown on What's Being Downloaded

There are two separate issues regarding the Internet and work: *lost productivity* and *accessing inappropriate content*. Both issues are of critical importance and should be included in any company's Internet-use policy. What may complicate matters somewhat is the fact that if an employee is *addicted* to the Internet than he may qualify for consideration under the *American's with Disabilities Act* (ADA). This makes dealing with such cases more complex. Employers should consult with their human resources and labor law specialist regarding this issue. If you're an employer, you may not be able to simply fire an employee for violating a company policy if he or she can demonstrate a legitimate psychological problem or illness, which Internet addiction may qualify as! This may also be true for those individuals who are addicted to pornography or other sexual behaviors. Sex addiction or sexually-compulsive behavior is a very real problem, with very real consequences.

Even if the Internet isn't addictive to most people, it's *highly stimulating* and fun to use and this translates into the potential for the abuse of time at home and at work! There are several key elements that make the Net problematic for both the employer and employee.

- *The Internet is a daily work tool.* The Internet is viewed as a work-related tool, and as such there is a greater potential tolerance of abusing it on the job. It can often be a part of daily routines, and therefore harder to avoid if it begins to become a problem.
- *Acceptability.* Using the computer is expected and considered desirable at work and there are many positive

reinforcements for the use of the Internet in performing a job, including efficiency and convenience.

- *Accessibility.* Computers are available virtually everywhere in the workplace. There are often out of the way places where terminals and PCs can be accessed, allowing for addictive or inappropriate use.

- *Immediacy.* The Net can usually be instantly accessed at work and is often available at high speed/broad bandwidth connections. A general rule of thumb for determining the addictive potential for a particular substance or a behavior, is that the *faster* the drug or stimulating behavior is absorbed or experienced, the greater the potential for addiction!

- *Difficult to monitor.* There is no easy way to reliably monitor the use or abuse of the Internet at work. Even in the companies that do monitor Web site access, it is usually done randomly, or with variable enforcement (although new software may change this). Many companies don't have a clear procedure for dealing with violations of their policy, which can be a problem when compliance is being questioned.

- *No specific Internet policies.* Although most businesses with Internet access *do not* have a clear Internet use policy, they typically *do* have some policy, either written or unwritten, regarding the use of company time for personal business. Because the Internet can use so much time from a workday, this becomes an even more critical issue when dealing with the potential problems of overusing the Net.

- *Time.* Even the average Internet user admits to being on the Net *much* longer than they initially plan to, *most* of the time. It's therefore very likely that most people who use the Net at work are overusing it, perhaps even for work-related activities. People report that even if they're going online to check one thing, they find themselves "stuck" online longer than they had intended. There are many reasons why this occurs, including dissociation, endless boundaries, and timelessness, but largely, it's because there are *no natural pauses* or *breaks* in acquiring the information you want. There is always more to find, another link to click, and that always takes more time!

Employers: Workplace Warning Signs of Internet Addiction

The following guidelines should serve as suggestions for employers in recognizing and addressing Internet problems with their employees. They should serve as guidelines only. Your human resources staff and an attorney should always review new personnel policies. Please note that using the computer or the Net a great deal at work isn't necessary a problem, it is when the use is *not* work-related and/or begins to interfere with work performance that it is a problem.

How to Spot a Nethead

Does your employee

- Spend what appears to be *excessive* amounts of time at their computer terminal beyond what would be expected to perform their job?
- Seem to be "clicking" to minimize or maximize something on their screen in your presence. They may actually be surfing Web pages and then closing the page when someone walks by. They may actually be surfing personal sites, including pornography sites. There are many stories of employees scanning for pornography all day, downloading it at work, and then taking it home for later use. Sometimes the photos are left on the hard drive at work, and can be discovered later.

Anyone could simply click on this material and accidentally view it?
- Experience excessive absences, tardiness, or a reduction in work output or productivity?
- Talk about the Internet all the time *or* remain silent about it, seeming to avoid the topic?
- Have adult, X-rated, or pornographic material that has been discovered on the screen or as saved downloads?
- Experience unexplained personal problems, such as: divorce, financial crisis, or physical illness? These can be due to problems related to Internet addiction, and should be discussed with your employee, following your normal personnel procedures.
- Appear to be unusually irritable and moody, particularly when not using the Internet or computer? There may be marked signs of depression, sadness, or social isolation, which can be signs of heavy Internet use or withdrawl (though they can be caused by numerous other reasons as well).
- Compulsively check their e-mail? There have been reports of people checking e-mail day and night, thirty or forty times a day! This can obviously waste a lot of time at work (and at home) and can compulsively repeat unless help is provided. Many employees report feeling compelled to continue this pattern even though it may be interfering with their work.

All of these symptoms can be caused or explained by other reasons besides the Internet. The point is to be aware of the possibility and make a referral to the company Employee Assistance Program (EAP) program if there is a notable disruption in work patterns. It should not be assumed that any problem with job performance is Internet-related; rather, this should serve to heighten your awareness of the issue.

What Can a Company Do?

First and foremost, a company should develop an Internet use policy at work. Be sure to clarify what the Web is used for while at work, and what your companies e-mail and download policies are.

- Display "Internet Use Policies" alongside the company "ADA" and "Sexual Harassment" guidelines.
- Clarify what the policy is regarding exposing coworkers to sexually objectionable material, including downloaded pornography.
- Identify and communicate the consequences of violating company Internet policy to all employees, supervisors, managers, and executives.
- Educate all supervisors, administrators, and managers about Internet abuse and addiction.
- Provide written material regarding the Internet policy to *all* employees, including the warning signs for Internet abuse and addiction.
- Consider installing a system to monitor Web traffic on the company Internet or network. Employees should be notified of whatever system you have in place and be fully informed as to the implications of violating use policies.
- Offer an Employee Assistance Program (EAP) to help deal with any personal or addiction problem that may interfere with job performance.

Why Should Your Company Have an EAP?

Facts:

- Approximately 7 out of 10 workers feel that stress has made them less productive.

- Between 10 and 23 percent of United States workers use drugs on the job.
- Studies have estimated that up to 60 percent of visits to doctors are for the "worried well."
- There is a 43 percent greater absenteeism for employees who use drugs and alcohol.
- In a study at the McDonnell Douglas Corporation, there was a 60 percent reduction in turnover for employees who sought mental health services through EAP, as well as a substantial reduction in medical claims costs.

Solutions:

- There is a 5:1 return on investment for EAP costs with 85 percent of the savings due to decreased medical claims. Many illnesses are stress related and can be appropriately assessed and treated with an EAP program.
- A 1990 study found that for every EAP dollar spent there was a $5–$16 savings.
- In recent studies, there were 14 fewer sick days after an EAP program was implemented. Average mental health and substance abuse claims costs were also reduced by 23 percent.
- Studies show a 37 percent reduction in medical costs after even brief counseling interventions.
- The Americans with Disability Act (ADA), the drug-free workplace, drug testing, ethnic and cultural diversity, workman's compensation claims, violence in the workplace, sexual harassment, various addictions including the Internet, and increased health care costs all have an impact on your companies profitability.

Most EAP companies can work closely with your company to develop an Employees Assistance Program (EAP) that will best suit your unique needs. A program can be created to ideally complement your existing medical plan and reduce unnecessary and increased insurance claims and additional costs, while dealing with problems that affect employee performance. Company size shouldn't be an obstacle as many EAP companies offer a flexible approach to designing your EAP program, and are able to service both large and small companies alike. Many have groups of counselors and specialists throughout the United States, as well as locally, and can meet with your employees near their homes or workplace.

Because fee structures are based on the number of employees and services you desire for your company, an EAP program can be affordable to the employer. Many EAP companies will charge on an "as needed basis" or will offer a flat rate based on the number of employees you have. Typically EAP services are available to all immediate family members living in the home at no extra charge to the *employer* or the *employee*! Employers can find out more about EAP services by contacting the Employee Assistance Professionals Association in Alexandria, Virginia.

Help for *You*, as an Employee and a Nethead

First, be clear that you do have a problem. To find out, you can take one of the self-tests in this book (chapters 3 and 4) or see a psychologist or other mental health professional. If your company does have an Employee Assistance Program (EAP), consider using it. It is *free* to all employees and their families, and most importantly it's *confidential*. Your employer need not know if you use the service. Names are not typically given to your employer about who attends and who does not.

If your online time is interfering with your work, you may want to speak with both the EAP counselor, as well as your immediate supervisor. The EAP counselor can also serve as an advocate if there are serious problems with your work as a result of your Internet abuse or addiction. Sometimes the company human resources specialist can help you deal with a work performance problem and act as an intermediary between you and your supervisor. It is perhaps best to weigh all your options prior to any action, although the EAP counselor or psychologist should be able to help guide you. You may wish to consult with a professional prior to speaking to your immediate supervisor.

If you violated a company policy, you may need to contact your union representative (if you have one) or you may wish to speak to an attorney specializing in labor relations. You should also consider utilizing the EAP program if one is available. If an EAP isn't available, consult with a private psychologist or other mental health professional. This may not necessarily be a serious problem for your employer, as many employers wish to give employees a chance to deal with the situation prior to any disciplinary action, unless the guidelines require a clear action on the part of your employer. It is wise to become familiar with your company's Internet use policies.

The important thing to remember is that if you're addicted to or are abusing the Internet, you have a legitimate problem and there are avenues to obtain the help you require. The following suggestions can help as well:

- *Don't keep things a secret from your spouse or close friends.* They can help you to deal with you're situation and can help you feel better. Having a support system in place is critical in helping you deal with any problem.

- *Consider joining a support group that deals with Internet addiction.*

- *Read about this problem and learn more about it.* There are numerous Web Sites and several books on the subject, which can be of tremendous help. Take note of the Resources section in the back of this book.

- *Create a password for your Internet access at work.* Give it to a trusted friend or therapist.

- *If you have any other addictions, try to deal with those as well.* There seems to be a strong correlation in having more than one addiction. There also may be underlying psychological issues that may contribute to your addiction problem. If you do not deal with other addictions or problems you have then they can act as a trigger to your Internet problem, leading to a repetition of the whole cycle. It is therefore important that if you work with a psychologist or other professional that he or she be familiar with addictions (preferably Internet addiction) as well as work-related issues.

Follow the guidelines in chapters 9 and 10 for more detailed suggestions on Internet addiction.

The Internet is definitely going to be a growing part of most workplaces in the future. As access speed increases and costs continue to drop, more and more business will be conducted via the Internet. Eventually, I predict most businesses will have some component of their work done through the Internet. This means that more and more workers will be exposed to the Internet. Progress must involve the inevitable pitfalls of any new technology, and there will undoubtedly be an increase in Internet-related problems, including addiction, in the workplace. If we can learn to address these issues now, we can assure that the Internet will continue to have a productive role to play in business and industry.

10

Cyberbalance

How to Enjoy and Benefit from Technology Without Being Consumed by It

Sometimes more is less, and less is more.

There is little doubt that technology helps us live our lives in better and more efficient ways. It can streamline otherwise tedious jobs, make boring tasks quicker, and save valuable human resources for more creative and pleasurable endeavors. There is, however, a price we pay for this efficiency: *stress.*

There is growing evidence that stress has a very real effect on our mental and physical well-being. Research suggests that levels of cortisol (a neurohormone) actually increase when we're exposed to continuous and uncontrolled sensory stimulation. In the book *Technostress*, psychologists Dr. Michelle Weil and Dr. Larry Rosen discuss how living in a high-tech, high-stress world can contribute to a variety of physical and psychological symptoms. The phenomenon of living in a world that never shuts off, and that continually bombards you with information calling for action, can definitely lead to burnout. Unless we begin to address how we can monitor, and if necessary change, the effects of technology on our lives, we can expect to experience negative effects to our health.

Too Much of a Good Thing

On average, we are exposed to significantly more communications input on a daily basis than at any previous time in our history. You need only look around at the beepers, cell phones, telephones, Internet, palm pilots, TV, radio, e-mail, voice mail, newspapers, snail mail, faxes, and more, incessantly bombarding us with urgent messages and coaxing us to respond. This constant state of arousal and stimulation comes from a daily unrelenting pressure to attend, listen, and act at a moment's notice. Remaining in this constant state of availability and readiness requires considerable mental and physical energy, which can lead to *fatigue, irritability, anxiety,* and *depression.* We also suffer a host of lifestyle problems, such as *overeating, TV addiction, compulsive spending,* and *drug* and *alcohol abuse.*

Internet abuse may be simply the latest means by which we comfort ourselves, which can become addictive. Under a constant pressure to respond, one is never "off-line." Downtime is *necessary* to recharge your human batteries (along with your lithium rechargeables)! The essential downtime we need has been eroded constantly by our ability to carry things such as beepers, cell phones, and palm pilots. We're always reachable, always accountable, and therefore, always stressed. Though we're engineered to handle stress, and in fact in small doses it can enhance our performance, we're not designed to handle this degree of stress on a prolonged basis. We must take steps to minimize the destructive impact of technology on our lives in order to remain balanced and healthy.

The Latest and Greatest

Many view the Internet as a wonderful new technology, which promises many great things, but not without a cost. The Internet is filled with wonderful potential and will undoubtedly reshape the world's economy and daily lives! Just look at the stock market to see how much excitement and faith we have in this newest form of communication. If a stock has Internet in it (or near it), it has got to be good. From the lessons learned from other new technologies we must realize that even something as seemingly innocuous as the Net has the potential for harm. It is therefore not surprising that many people are reporting *increased stress* and *addiction* related to their Internet use.

Technical progress can never be benign, and all scientific advancements carry their requisite price. This only seems logical, for everything that has benefit must also have a cost. It is this collective denial of potential harm that renders any new technology as dangerous. Technology is one-dimensional, but real-time living is three-dimensional and, as such, encompasses the essence of our humanity. If we remember this, we'll use and develop technology with *safety* and *balance*.

High-Tech Living

We're just beginning to realize that there are very palpable economic and psychological costs to high-tech living, not the least of which is the constant pressure to keep up with a technology that changes every four months! You never gain a sense of mastery or peace when the landscape is never the same twice. You should begin to ask yourself if the latest *high-speed processor* is really that necessary. After being promised so many times that this latest version or system will become "the standard" we've become skeptical. It's an endless cycle.

Is the latest truly the greatest? Not only are you oversaturated with high-tech pressure, but it's impossible to not fall behind the technology curve. This can leave you feeling continually frustrated. Many of us end up walking around with *perpetual processor envy*! This tech-trap is easy to become ensnared in because each new advance promises greater possibilities, seducing you with new applications. Many of these new possibilities never materialize, or if they do, they take far longer to become practical than originally promised. Even if the product is as promised, is it improved enough to justify the additional time lost, as well as the stress?

Emerging from the Net: How to Free Yourself

This chapter offers ways to recognize the signs and symptoms of high-tech stress-out and provides methods to deal with the acute and ongoing problems related to Internet technology. From the work I do with my patients and corporate clients, I can see that, as alluring as technology can be, it *cannot* replace the quality and touch of human relationships. Our true health and vitality come from these interpersonal, not online, relationships. Even the social aspects of the Internet, including e-mail and chat rooms, do not equal the real connections that people require to remain psychologically healthy.

It seems that *real-time human interaction* is hard-wired into our genetic makeup. We know this from a long history of health and behavioral research on physical and social contact. Indeed, most of us recognize that when we remain socially isolated for an extended period of time, we experience symptoms of depression and other problems. In extreme cases a loss of reality testing can occur, which can lead to psychosis. People who spend excessive amounts of time alone often report such alterations in their behavior, and we all have heard the severe cases of loners who end up committing antisocial acts (Unabomber, the Oklahoma bombings, Columbine H.S., etc.).

In short, we need social contact to stay mentally healthy. We probably also need human connections to survive physically.

We Need Human Interaction

There was a landmark study done many years ago that demonstrated this point. Children in an orphanage were divided into two groups: one group was given all physical and psychological requirements for survival. They provided food, water, milk, and rest, along with attention, holding, and playing in a loving manner. The second group of infants were given the physical requirements only. They were *not* given the touching and tenderness, which the first group received. The results were staggering. Although such research would never be conducted today, they found that many of the children in the second, physical-only group died, while their emotionally fed counter parts went on to thrive. The only difference was the degree of love and social contact given!

I also believe that social interaction is part of our genetic map for survival. It's necessary for us as social animals to utilize *social interdependence* in order to survive as a species. Although we are shielded from our daily interdependence by our modern society, without social cooperation we undoubtedly could not survive!

Is Your Mouse Really Your Friend?

In spite of the countless claims of a renewed social life as the result of the Internet, recent studies are actually beginning to show that there may be a decline in social interaction and positive mood as a result of too much time cyber-relating. This is not to say people cannot benefit socially from the Internet. They certainly can and do. I have personally read hundreds of e-mail testimonials on the miracle of the Net in their lives. One patient described her Internet contacts as "a ray of sunshine" for her. For some people the Internet serves as good practice for real-time social interactions. The key word here is *practice*, for many, if not most (around 30 percent), of the people who meet online seem to progress their relationship to more personal modes of communication such as the telephone or real-time contact. This indicates that we continue to need a more direct connection to other people to achieve a *sense of balance, grounding,* and *perspective*. People like and want high tech, but they need *high touch* experiences to remain healthy and vital.

Catching Your Balance

Like it or not, we are complex organisms who require a delicate balance between the *physical, psychological, social,* and *spiritual* aspects of our humanity. This *balance,* or homeostasis, is critical in remaining healthy. We're not integrated circuits. Even *Star Trek,* while depicting a technically advanced humanity, portrays an emphasis on human interaction and a sense of balance. Their starships have psychological counselors available, not a computer program or holographic facsimile! *High tech can never replace social connection.*

Technology, whether it is the Internet or a DVD player, has the inherent potential to either help balance, or upset the equilibrium of our lives. This occurs when we give it subtle (or overt) leverage on our time and energy. New technology is in our faces every day promising us a better life. But technology is only an advance if it actually *improves* the *quality* of our lives. Quality implies the inclusion of *all aspects* of a balanced life— the physical, emotional, social, and spiritual aspects of our being.

Technology does not serve us well in maintaining this kind of balance. We give the Internet our time and energy that *is therefore no longer available to other more social aspects of our lives.* Even as I write this book, I feel the Internet calling my attention as I frequently take e-mail breaks during my writing sessions. I also remain acutely aware that the time I spend e-mailing, surfing, and working on my Web pages is time I am *not* spending with my wife and children, exercising, or doing other productive and important activities in my life. If I allowed it to happen, I could spend several hours a day cyber-surfing or working on my Web sites, which would delay my bedtime, reduce my sleep, and interfere with my parenting responsibilities the next morning (not to mention angering my wife!). Even now, as I edit this chapter, I'm doing so on my laptop while my wife drives the car with our two children in their car seats in back. Not to mention the cell phone, two beepers, PDA, and TV/VCR we have in the car as we drive home from a weekend away. I often write this book while my children sleep, so I can be available to them later, but it is a definite juggling act. So even though I am a tech junkie (I know it and I'm not proud), I consciously maintain some degree of balance in my life. It may not be easy, but it's worth it.

Time Online, or Time in Life?

Let's face it, technology eats up time, and the Internet's time-distorting properties are particularly good at unbalancing other parts of our lives that call for our time and energy. Again, whenever you spend inordinate amounts of time online, you are *not* spending time on the other important parts of your life. It isn't the act of being online that is so damaging necessarily. Rather, it's the loss of other essential parts of our humanity as a result of living in cyberland. It's also the fact that the Internet produces the *illusion* of *intimacy*, when in fact it can be very one-dimensional. Although many people report experiencing significant relationships with those whom they met online, it is difficult to determine how the Internet uniquely contributes to the development of a relationship.

Mental health experts are beginning to question whether the Internet provides a haven for those who suffer from *chronic shyness, social phobias*, or other *interpersonal problems*. The Internet may simply prolong such difficulties for some people. Balance, then, can only occur where there is *flexibility* in how you spend your time. When you feel you have a choice, as opposed to a compulsion (or avoidance), to make some aspect of your life a bit easier, you have *balance in your life*.

You Are What You Do, so Change How You Do It

There are many ways to combat the impact of high-tech heaven, which is particularly hard for us technophiles who love the stuff. There's nothing like a new gadget to brighten your day. I believe a great deal of the phenomenal performance of the Internet stocks is due to the fact that people love the whole concept of the Internet and its related technology. People are attracted to the promise of this new technological frontier and it excites them to be a part of it. Excited people buy new gadgets based on this emotion. Time will prove the best test of this process, but there is no debating the intense interest this technology generates.

If you want to change how you feel, you have to change something you do. Feelings are based on our own actions. To change a negative pattern you must do something different. The use and abuse of any technology, including the Internet, requires an honest self-analysis, and a willingness to hear the answers you receive, and a willingness to change your behavior in some way.

How to Log Off and Log In to Yourself

The first step in getting off this high-tech merry-go-round is to recognize that you may be becoming too carried away by the Net. I received a call from a writer who felt he'd become addicted to e-mail. Sound absurd? Perhaps, but the fact was that he felt he was losing control over his *choices*, which is a sure sign of an addictive process.

Admitting that you're in an addictive cycle is the beginning of rebalancing your life. Hopefully, you won't need to hit bottom before you start to do something to change your life. Following are some key warning signs and suggestions to help keep you balanced in your approach to the Internet.

Signs and Suggestions for a Balance Overhaul

- *You find yourself thinking, reading, or talking about technology or the Internet all the time.* Find other interests and activities to get involved in. Do not let computers or the Internet become your only focus. Take some time to explore other interests, including physical activities. Remind yourself to talk about other things besides the Internet even if you find this the most interesting topic. Consider establishing friendships with people who have varying interests. Don't be afraid to ask questions and learn about new things.

- *You find that you shy away from casual social interactions and are avoiding real-time friends.* Take some time, at least once a week, to call or meet with a real-time friend. Preferably someone you haven't met online. Contact an old friend who you haven't seen for a while, perhaps someone who you knew before the cyberage began. Go low tech: take a walk, have a cup of coffee, go to a movie. Stretch your social muscles and force yourself to connect without the ease or distance of cyberspace. Consider joining a social organization or group, or take a class that will help you meet new people

- *You find yourself becoming more inpatient with people, and seem to have less tolerance for everyday stresses and pressure; people are describing you as becoming short-tempered and easily annoyed without apparent reason.* People are not as efficient as machines, but they're infinitely more gratifying. If you're reacting too intensely, you may be experiencing symptoms of stress. Your body and mind can usually cope with small variations in levels of stress but if it gets too great you may become irritable. If this happens to you, turn off the computer. Take a day with no technology in it. Don't even drive if you can avoid it. Live without TV. Just take a day, or even a half-day, to remind yourself that you can live without the joys and stresses of technology. Ignore your e-mail; let it sit in cyberspace limbo for a day or so. It will still be there for you to retrieve. Remember that the availability of the technology doesn't mean you have to access it *every day*. When you can *choose* when and where you wish to partake, you are no longer at the mercy of the Net. Technology will then be serving you, on more human terms.

One person described to me getting up at five A.M., feeling compelled to check his e-mail! This is not rational, and is probably not necessary either. Nothing, for the most part, cannot wait until morning, or the next day! To have balance one must set limits and boundaries, and you cannot wait for someone else to do it for you, because they won't. You have to be the one to turn off the TV, log off the computer, or turn off your beeper. The act of doing so creates a small stand for your *humanity*, and reminds you and the rest of the world that there is more to life than can be reduced to digital bites!

- *You are experiencing more frequent colds, aches and pains, or other physical symptoms.* There is a direct correlation between our emotional health and our immune functions, so any increase in stress, along with associated elevations in cortisol, can have the "Net effect" of increasing your vulnerability to illness. There is also a tendency for people to "somatize" stress by expressing their stress through physical symptoms. In other words, you may not realize you're stressed, tired, or lonely, but you may feel tension headache. It's easier in many cultures to admit to having a physical symptom than an emotional one! Talking to people in real-time can help. There's something very therapeutic about connecting with another human being that reduces stress. Seeing a psychologist or therapist might also help deal with some of the toxic aspects of modern living. I believe the more "high tech" we become, the more "high touch" we will *need to* become to compensate.

Finally, consider getting a pet. Here is a very low-tech solution to cyberlife. Animals help ground us, and connect us to something beyond ourselves. There is good evidence to suggest that pets can lower blood pressure, heart rate, and promote well-being in their owners. Pet therapy is used with seniors in nursing homes to help keep them emotionally healthy, which again translates to better physical health!

- *Work or school has become less important to you and/or your performance has deteriorated.* Balance technology with the key areas of your life, such as work and school. There are many stories of people spending hours a day online at work, or staying home from school just to surf the Web, e-mail, or chat online! Each central area of our life must be given weight in order to stay balanced. Again, this means saying "no" sometimes, and in the case of the Internet, you're usually saying "no" to yourself! But you're also saying "yes" to real-time life.

- *You find yourself using alcohol, drugs, or other addictive behaviors, including compulsive Internet use, food, sex, shopping, gambling, or work.* There seems to be a strong correlation among various addictions and addiction to the Internet. Our research shows that many Internet addicts also demonstrated other forms of addictive or compulsive behavior. It is important that you recognize any tendency toward becoming addicted to other behaviors and to seek professional help if you feel you have begun to lose control of some of those behaviors.

There are many twelve-step support groups to deal with most addictions and problems, including Alcoholics Anonymous, Narcotics Anonymous, Cocaine Anonymous, Overeaters Anonymous, Gamblers Anonymous, Compulsive Spending and Shopping groups, and others. The Resources section at the back of the book lists many of these groups. Getting the support of your friends and family to assist you, along with a psychologist or other therapist, can be of immeasurable help as well if you're dealing with multiple addictions.

- *You find yourself feeling pressured to own the latest software version, newest hardware, or latest gadget and feel frustrated when you cannot do so.* I call this *processor envy*—when you feel the continual pull to improve and increase you technological power by upgrading. The problem is there is no end in sight due to the rapidity of changes. I was recently ordering a new desktop computer. Instinctively I ordered the latest processor, without even knowing anything about it. I just assumed if it was newer, it was better. This is the trap, and the illusion. I chose to force myself *not* to get the best. The new processor is probably better, but how much so, and at what financial and psychological costs. By wanting, or needing, to get the latest or greatest technology you set a dangerous precedent of endless upgrades (with no sense of true satisfaction). You are also feeding the illusion of there always being something better. This pattern creates a chronic state of frustration, which does not, in my opinion, add a lot of quality to your life.

- *You believe that you can "master" the Internet or other technology and you're quite frustrated by the reality that you cannot.* You must approach the mastery of the Internet or other technology from the perspective of a process, as opposed to an outcome. It is illusory to try to gain mastery of a process that changes almost daily.

You can only hope to achieve a healthy balance in your technical life by acknowledging the fact that the best you can hope for is to be in the *process of learning,* while never mastering it.

- *Your relationship with your loved one has become strained, and you feel alienated from each other.* When you use *leftover time* for a marriage you get leftover results. When you spend hours each day online or on the computer, you're *not* spending it with your spouse or lover and that *has* to have a negative impact on your relationship! Relationships are a process (not a processor) and as such it requires time and attention in order for it to feel vital. It is difficult to be intimate with two people at once, and the Internet or computer can, at times, feel like a second person. Balance in a relationship involves giving your significant other at least some standing on your busy (and sometimes misplaced) list of priorities. There is certainly room for the Internet in a marriage or relationship, but only if there's room for the marriage and the Internet!

The problems and solutions I've suggested should serve as markers along the delicate path toward balance in your life. The list is by no means exhaustive. There are probably as many perils as there are promises and all require a commitment to creating a harmony with our cyberlives and our real lives. We usually know, on some level, when our world is out of balance. Sometimes, this knowledge comes from the feedback of others, but it always requires listening to your heart and soul and by taking the *chance to change.* It's up to you to initiate change. When it comes to Internet addiction and high-tech stress, the only thing harder than *changing,* is *not* changing.

11

Cyberkids

How to Safeguard Your Child from Harm Online

*Children are the mirrors to our past,
and the portals to our future.*

Anyone who has children old enough to use the computer and the Internet knows the horror (and embarrassment) felt when they realize that their children know their way around the computer better than they do. The computer, including the Internet, is our children's technology, and they have an intuitive grasp of the medium. Today's children are *multimedia-responsive*, and the Internet offers a virtual multimedia experience at the push of a button. They approach new computer skills and challenges more easily than their pre-digital parents and, as such, are likely to make forays into the darker side of cyberspace with little awareness of their safety.

Children also use the Internet for their social meeting place to talk, gossip, and just "hang out." The Net is the equivalent of the shopping mall—the virtual mall for the new age. It offers anonymity, stimulation, fun, sex, and intrigue. You put all this together and you get a highly attractive venue for teenagers.

I had two parents in my office recently. They were divorced, and we were there to talk about parenting skills and their child's behavior. Toward the end of our conversation, the mother brought up a question I hadn't been asked before. Without knowing about this book, she asked me about her son's Internet behavior, and what she should watch out for. This began a discussion on taking steps to decrease some of the inherent risk found online. Her question was a good one and it is likely to be asked many times in coming years.

Children can easily access information about sex, weapons, bomb making and, with some creativity, even purchase liquor, pornography, and guns. If a child has the tenacity, they can get virtually anything they want. Unfortunately, children and teens may lack the judgment and/or healthy fear to avoid such information and products.

Change Is Only Progress if It Truly Improves the Quality of Our Lives

The purpose of this chapter is *not* to alert parents to the evils of the Internet, nor to extol its virtual virtues, but rather to offer some information and guidelines to teach parents and children safe habits for using this wonderful and potent tool.

We know that the computer and the Internet offer an incredible array of information and opportunity for our children. The available *information, resources,* and *references* are truly unimaginable by baby boomer standards, and while we may think some of it comes too easy, the truth is, our children will have a facility with the world's information, unparalleled in history. Unlike TV, the Net fosters an exciting interaction with information, which they consume in the form of text, visual images, and sound. Although it shares some of the same features as TV, it is clearly much more. It is the added interactivity, ease of access, twenty-four-hour availability, and anonymity that make the Internet so powerful and potentially harmful if not monitored adequately.

There is likely to be a continuum of problems and challenges that face children and the Internet. At the most basic are general safety issues related to *how* and *when* your child accesses the Internet. Misuse can lead to abuse. The goal is to alert parents and concerned adults of the potential of abuse and the possibility of an addiction. A child can become addicted to the Net, although it may be less obvious than with an adult. Not every child who likes to spend time online is going to get addicted; rather, they may at times find themselves misusing the Net. This can escalate to more severe difficulties in the future.

Internet Legislation

Many of you may be familiar with the 1996 Communications Decency Act, which was struck down as unconstitutional by the Supreme Court. It was the government's first attempt to control/limit material on the Internet. In 1999, the Child Online Protection Act is the latest attempt to try to effectively ban cyberporn and other objectionable material in order to protect our children. There have been several court rulings that have ostensibly upheld the rights and responsibilities of free speech for most anything on the Internet. Such freedoms include pornography and other adult material that children can access online.

There are some exceptions, as in the recent case where a judge ruled that a pro-life Web site could not continue to display information that was suggestive of violence. The issues of balancing free speech against censorship and safety are indeed complex. In spite of software filtering programs and parental controls, along with disclaimers on the sites themselves, children often find their way in to sites that they clearly shouldn't be viewing.

Part of the problem is that many Web sites (especially porn sites) send out thousands of unsolicited e-mails that are disguised link invitations to their adult site. I demonstrated this to the parents I mentioned earlier, who also didn't know that their child could access the most objectionable material by simply dialing a 900 line, receiving an access code, and viewing the paid-for material. Although 900 lines aren't permitted to allow minors to gain access, there is no way for the 900 line to know your child's age. The screening programs on your online service provider often won't pick these up because the Spammed (junk) messages do not contain any hint of pornographic reference in their topic. You can, however, block 900 line access on your phone.

When you view a junk e-mail topic, all you see is a message that sounds important. This leads you to open up the message. Your child is likely to do the same and they may find themselves logging on to an adult site *without ever intending to do so*. There is very toxic sexual information on the Web, some of which can be quite shocking and unsettling. With the exception of monitoring your child's Internet use, it's difficult to stop the infiltration of such information completely.

Sexploitation on the Internet

Unfortunately there are also those people online who use the Internet to exploit children and adolescents. Just today, in my home state of Connecticut, there was a news story of a twelve-year-old child who was found meeting a thirty-one-year-old man with whom she'd been communicating on the Net. During an interview by a local TV news reporter, I was asked what a twelve-year-old girl could want from a thirty-one-year-old man. The answer is almost too simple: attention, excitement, and intimacy, which are what many people want in some fashion.

Seventy-five percent of Internet addicts surveyed admitted to intense feelings of intimacy when online, and nearly 40 percent of nonaddicted Netheads report strong feelings of intimacy as well. This young girl chose to use the Internet to make powerful connections with people, but online it is very difficult to evaluate someone's motives, honesty, or intent. You can't even verify someone's age or even gender for that matter! The phenomenon of accelerated intimacy I discussed earlier is easy to see here, for when you spend four hours a day for weeks on end talking to someone online, you *do* develop a form of intimacy. Although somewhat limited in its focus, it is still an intensive form of human communication, and can develop at a much more rapid rate as compared to other forms of communication. The problem is that you never know what is true and what isn't, and our research indicates that about *half* the people online do admit to lying online. This certainly makes it difficult to evaluate someone's integrity. Until someone can figure out how to verify what we're told online (and that is probably coming soon), we must use some sensible precautions.

Beware of Sexual Predators

Because there are sexual predators in the world, and unfortunately they too have discovered the many uses of the Internet, you must demonstrate some degree of suspicion toward all unknown people your child communicates with online. The Net makes no judgments and is universally accessible to all (which is part of its essence and attraction) who seek access. There are those who will surf the chat rooms looking for children to start a conversation with, and a child will often welcome a stranger paying exclusive attention to them when picked from dozens of others in a particular chat room. Most of these are males looking for young girls or boys, sometimes even disguising themselves to impersonate a peer with the hopes of developing a relationship. Sometimes, such online relationships will extend the cyber-relationship to the telephone or personal meetings.

The following chart offers a snapshot of the types of sexual behavior that people engage in online. Online sexual behavior doesn't necessarily remain online. Among Internet addicts there appears to be a progression from the virtual to the actual. The following table describes the progression of sexual behavior from online to real-time, comparing Internet addicted versus nonaddicted percentages.

Online Behavior	Nonaddicted	Addicted
Flirting	20 percent	57 percent
Explicit Sex-Talk	9 percent	38 percent
Masturbation	12 percent	37 percent
Online affair	14 percent	42 percent
Phone contact	18 percent	50 percent
Real-time sex	13 percent	31 percent

The data suggest that there is a continuum of online sexual behavior, which appears to be significantly higher for those who are Internet addicted. This suggests the need for further study to examine the interrelationship between Internet addiction, online sexual behavior, and sexual addiction. There also appears to be a correlation between online affairs leading to phone contact and eventual in-person sex.

Childhood Immortality and Danger

Children often have no real conception of danger, and may at times be intrigued by it. They lack experience, which when coupled with a sense of immortality, produces a *willingness to take unnecessary risks*. We spend years trying to teach our children to look beyond the present, in order to allow them to see the implications of their behavior. Care has be to taken, however, in not glamorizing the danger, thereby making the Net more attractive. Rather, a better approach must be to *monitor* and *limit* your child's Internet time and activities, while gently educating them on its uses and abuses. I will also offer some general precautions as well as ways of structuring your children's time online to help minimize any inherent risks at the end of this chapter.

Connecting to the World

When your children connect to the Internet, they're literally connecting to the world, and potentially everyone in it! Clearly, this can be a wonderfully expansive opportunity, but it can also be dangerous. You must exercise the same cautions in allowing your children to spend time online as you would concerning other activities. Although you wouldn't let your child roam the streets alone at night unsupervised, this is essentially what you're doing when you let your children go online without knowing anything about where they're going. For example, there are ways for your child to access hardcore adult material by calling an adult Web site's membership registration fee into a 900 line. The phone doesn't know that your child is under eighteen years old, and after the fee is charged to your phone bill, they have open access to every type of sex imaginable. You may be able to reverse the charge on the phone bill, but by the time you see the bill they will have had access to the Web site. Even without a credit card or 900-access number, your child can enter a world of dangerous information about sex, violence, hate propaganda, firearms, alcohol, and other sensitive subjects.

Computer and Internet Video Games

Any parent who has children over four or five years old is aware of the popularity of computer and video games. They are a significant part of the lives of many children. One need not look very hard to see the prevalence of game systems such as Nintendo, Sega, and Sony Play Station. These latest iterations of computer entertainment technology are far more interactive and realistic. They have advanced graphics and audio capabilities, making them close to an interactive movie. They're so popular that one might be hard-pressed not to see the familiar (and latest) Color Game Boy several times a day if you're around children regularly. Indeed, some children seem to become almost addicted to these games, and parents are having to limit their use.

Progress never stops, however. Some of the latest game innovations are highly sophisticated interactive computer games that can be played by multiple players via the Net. You can have two or more children in different parts of the world playing the same game interactively! Some of these game sites require a fee; while for others there is a charge for the software, which is then played using the Internet. Games such as Multiple User Digital Domains (MUDDING) can be extraordinarily popular, creating a large and devoted following. And many of these games have stong themes of violence. These games are highly challenging, and can be quite *time-consuming*. Eventually, it seems likely that most video games will be either acquired or played interactively through the Internet.

We know that the Net will likely play a larger role in electronic games, as our research reports that almost 60 percent of computer time is spent playing games! As the costs of computer and video games decrease, there will probably be a continued increase in Internet-based games. You'll no longer need a willing partner and two joysticks; all you'll need is Web access and the world becomes your virtual partner and playground!

The more interactive the game, the more potentially addictive it seems to become. As video games have moved to the Internet, they allow yet another form of social interaction to become digitized instead of played out on, say, a basketball court. Although it's not necessarily negative to share such activities with peers online, there's no doubt that they can be so time-consuming that they can be abused. Children have been known to spend hours online playing games, often avoiding other responsibilities.

There are some positives about computer games. They may improve attention and concentration, eye/hand coordination, and fine motor skills. Sometimes we'll even prescribe such activities to assist children with attention problems such as ADD (Attention Deficit Disorder) or other learning disabilities. They can also be a lot of fun and quite intellectually challenging, requiring skills such as abstraction, motor speed, coordination, and reasoning skills.

Can My Child Be Addicted to the Net?

Connecting with undesirable people and logging on to X-rated Web sites aren't the only issues to be concerned about. Our research suggests that there is a very real potential for children to use the Internet abusively. *There is no reason to believe that children are immune to this potential.* Because the Internet can be such a socially isolating experience, there is great risk that overusing it may lead to your child missing out on important age-appropriate activities, such as friends, sports, homework, and family time.

It is not only that the Internet is inherently dangerous to your child (although certain precautions should be taken to minimize any risks), but rather when a child spends too much time online, there is the potential that they *could* become *addicted*. Even if they never become addicted, overuse or abuse can hamper your child's social, educational, and psychological development. This is perhaps the same precaution one might apply to using television excessively or inappropriately.

The Internet is a new technology and, as with all new technologies, problems arise that are often not anticipated. The Internet is no exception. Remember, it contains a virtual connection to all the world's information and people. The Internet is truly interactive, even if the user is unaware of this process. Most Web sites even have "cookies" connected to them where they can track your child's visit to the site, often for future marketing. Advertisers will also use this information to track your child's interests (and potential buying power) and will either sell your child's e-mail address and/or use it to push targeted products and services.

Guidelines for Parents

For children, it becomes critical to know whom and what they connect with in order to protect their welfare. On the Net there is a significant amount of information that can be inappropriate or damaging for your child to view. The following guidelines can hopefully assist you in safely negotiating this new cyberfrontier so your children may continue to enjoy the wonders the Internet offers.

- *Tell your children to never give out any identifying information online.* Don't let your child give out names, addresses, or phone numbers unless you know the person or have checked out the situation as you would with any new friend. You want to show the same attention to cyberfriends as you would any other real-time friend. This is not unlike insisting that your children not talk to strangers, or not to tell them where they live. If someone online insists on knowing information about your child, instruct them to inform you and cut off communication with the online person, at least until you know more about what's going on. We have to remember that children are inherently trusting, and they may not fully appreciate the potential danger of the Net.

- *Set your browser to not accept "cookies."* This will stop advertisers from capturing information about your child or your family. Some Web sites will not allow you to open their site unless you allow the "cookies" to be "eaten." This is their way of capturing valuable marketing data for future use in marketing to your account; it also allows them to sell your account information.

  The problem with this captured marketing has gotten so insidious that the Federal Trade Commission got involved in a dispute with a very popular Web site over engaging in deceptive advertising practices. Many consumer groups have reacted to this issue. Marc Rotenberg, director of the Electronic Privacy Information Center, predicted that marketing as we knew it, which targeted an age range, can now target a specific child, in a specific demographic group, in a particular community! Needless to say there are many people who are very concerned about this potential to manipulate and coerce our children toward certain products and services. Any parent knows the power of advertising already, as evidenced when their five-year-old asks for a toy that they saw on a TV show that morning!

- *Be aware of the safety issues when tying up your phone line while online.* When you use a dial-up access to the Internet, as most of us do, you're busying your phone line. When the modem is being used, you cannot receive phone calls or make them. There may be safety concerns with closing phone access to your home, especially when a parent isn't home. If there's an emergency, such as a fire or medical problem, calls cannot come in or go out, perhaps when most needed. It might be reasonable to limit access, especially when you're not home (which should be done anyway), or consider obtaining a second phone line or cable modem.

- *Consider blocking 900-line access in your home.* Web site purveyors have developed another way around using a credit card to charge membership or purchase products online. It works like this: Say your child accesses an adult Web site, which requires a fee. To pay that fee, they can call a 900 number that charges to your phone bill a set fee automatically (unless you have it blocked on your phone). Once the fee goes through, you instantly receive an automated message indicating your access code. You then hang up and enter that access code in the appropriate field on the Web site and you're in! The whole process takes about two minutes and unless you have the 900 line access and/or access to adult Web sites blocked, your child can easily get access to material you may not want him or her viewing.

- *Keep the computer in a public place in your home.* Try not to put the computer in your child's bedroom. If you do, make sure there is no Internet connection available there. Your child shouldn't be alone with the Net; this privacy can foster the autonomy and accelerated intimacy that often occurs in Internet relationships. Your child may rapidly begin to develop online relationships you know nothing about. Having the computer in a public place will discourage using the Net to communicate inappropriate information, or to engage in cyberflirting, cybersex, downloading adult material, or anything objectionable, and therefore enticing. Also consider creating a password to assess the Web that you, the parent, controls and limits access to.

- *Learn about the computer and the Internet.* Get to know the basics of the Internet if you want to be able to prevent problems for your children. Try to learn some of the Internet language and become familiar with the terms used online. There are courses available through most adult education programs and dozens of books on the subject, and of course you can always learn online. The more that you know about what your child is doing, the better able you'll be to monitor their online activities. Don't be afraid to ask questions that may seem silly to you. Ask your child to teach you about the Internet. Your interest will go a long way in building your relationship, as well as helping you to understand what your child is doing when they spend all that time online. It will also let your child know that you're watching, that you care, and that they cannot get away with anything inappropriate.

- *Limit you child's time online.* Try to set limits for the amount of time your child spends online just as you would for TV or video games. Too much of anything can create an inbalance in your child's development. The only way to monitor this is to set firm guidelines about how and when they can use the computer for games or Internet access. Don't be afraid to set limits and clear rules regarding the use of the Internet and be prepared to enforce consequences if they don't follow the rules. There are many positives about the Internet for children if guidance is applied.

- *Set the filters, child protections, and parental controls on your browser or Internet Service Provider (ISP).* There are parental control settings available on most ISPs to limit access to certain parts of the Internet and to help prevent access to unwanted material. I say limit because there's no 100 percent reliable way to prevent access. If you're unsure how to do this, ask your ISP. Even child protection software, such as Net Nanny, Cyber Patrol, and Cyber Tots are not foolproof. The best solution to this high-tech dilemma is a very low-tech one: supervise your child's activities online. Although you cannot be there all the time, something is better than nothing, and this attention reinforces that you care. You might want to set up a rule that there be no online use without a parent at home; although this may seem drastic, it communicates to your children a clear boundary. With older children you can relax the rules, as you become more confident about their Internet-use pattern.

- *Monitor your child's e-mail.* While you don't want to be too intrusive, you want to know something about what and with whom your child is talking online. There are hundreds of cases where parents are shocked to find out that their child was having an extended (and flirtatious) e-mail relationship with an adult. There are serious implications for these types of situations. Remember that the younger your child is, the less likely it is that they will recognize the potential risk of their e-mail activity. In some cases, children have made plans to meet these people, without the parent's knowledge, and there are several tragic stories where teens have been murdered! There are many cases where meetings have occurred without *any knowledge* by parents, which presents a serious potential risk for your children. Although it's important to respect your child's privacy, checking in with your child occasionally is appropriate in safeguarding them against the inherent risks of cyberspace.

- *Encourage your child to engage in other, real-time activities.* Even with the obvious educational value of the Internet (and there is a lot), there's still no better way to capture the imagination and creativity of your child than real-time reading. There is something special about reading actual books that creates a powerful and stimulating experience. This isn't necessarily better than the Internet, but it is an experience of a different depth. It can also be important to encourage sports, music, hobbies, spiritual/religious involvement, clubs, as well as other social activities. The Internet is a wonderful educational tool, but it can be a socially isolating and one-dimensional activity. There is richness in real-time social relationships that cannot be replicated online; this is why many online relationships seem to progress from the Internet to personal contact via the telephone or an actual meeting. There is definitely a place for the Internet in your child's life, but it should not be to the exclusion of other, more traditional social activities.

Just because your child likes the Internet does *not* mean they have a problem or that they are addicted! Many children enjoy computers and the Internet. Computer games, MUDDs, e-mail, and chat all offer unique and stimulating fun for your child. Internet use *only* becomes a problem when it is truly interfering with your child's daily life and activities. Do not be alarmed if your child fits a few of the warning signs noted here. However, some of the signs may serve as general indicators that something may be bothering your child which you should attend to.

Watch for signs of Internet addiction or abuse in your child, such as:

- Spending excessive or increasingly greater amounts of time online
- Ignoring other responsibilities in their life
- Decreasing grades or poor work performance
- Frequent absences from school or job
- Ignoring real-time friends in favor of new online relationships
- An unwillingness to talk about what they're doing online
- Increased irritability and social isolation
- Changes in mood, particularly depression
- Less interest in traditional activities he or she was previously involved in
- Meeting or telephoning new people they met online

Become familiar with these warning signs when monitoring your child's Internet use. Trust your gut reaction. If you see your child spending eight hours a day online and neglecting friends or other activities, you should try talking about it together first. Take the time to educate your child and to set boundaries for Internet use. If that doesn't work, you may want to seek some help from a psychologist or other therapist with experience in treating children. This is not to say that spending a lot of time online is necessarily bad, rather it is the potential exclusion of other activities that are important to your child's health that is of concern. *Remember, spending time online means you're not spending time doing something else,* and it is the exclusion of these other activities that can cause psychological damage to your child's life. Some kids love computers and the Internet and you don't want to discourage a real hobby or interest (who knows, your child might be the next Bill Gates). Just try to use your judgment in maintaining balance for your child, while taking into account the positives and negatives of computers and the Internet.

- **Do not store sensitive information or photos in the family computer if you don't want your child to see them.** There may be information about work, finances, or sexually-related material that you don't want your child to view, and if the information is available on the machine your child may find it. Remember, children have an ease with computers we adults often don't have. They'll look in your personal folders and files. Remember that everything you store in a hard drive can be recovered if you know your way around the computer. Children are innately curious, and a bit nosy (especially when it comes to their parents), and they will hack around the computer exploring until they find something. They often know more about the computer than you, and may know a few hacking "tricks" that you didn't know.

More Tips on Safeguarding Your Child

Parents should monitor their child's access to the Internet just as they would with TV or any other activity. There's no shortcut to protecting your children from cyberspace; you must take an active role in protecting, monitoring, and limiting what your children will have access to. Here are some guidelines to help a parent negotiate cyberspace safely.

- *Be familiar with the computer and the Internet.* Don't be strangers to this new technology. Even if you don't like computers, you should become familiar with them. If you don't know what's going on, you're more likely to have your kids become involved in something without your knowledge.
- *Don't be afraid to ask your children questions about what they're doing.* Question them on what they are viewing online and routinely monitor their use patterns, e.g., how long they spend online and what sites they visit.
- *Check your hard drive for downloaded files of material that you might find objectionable or inappropriate for you child to see.* Don't be bashful! You have to be willing to be a little nosy at times. Don't confuse appropriate interest and caution on your part with overinvolvement. Obviously, you don't want to be intrusive, and what you do and say should be appropriate to your child's age. Being too intrusive in your teenager's life is different than looking over your eight-year-old's shoulder, but reasonable involvement is necessary in both cases. Do not ignore troubling or suspicious information or behavior!
- *Sit down with your child and talk to them about responsible use of the Internet and to limit access if you feel they're not using the powerful medium appropriately.* The Internet is not benign. Because the Web is connected to everything, you need to decide if you want your child to have unlimited access to everything. This doesn't apply only to sexually-related sites, but to other information that may not be suitable to your child's age as well; you may have to monitor or control Web access

to certain areas to limit the potential for viewing questionable material.

- *Take notice of any unusual changes in your child's behavior.* Look for changes in eating and sleeping habits; pay particular attention to their social patterns. You want to note if they're becoming less social and more isolated. The Internet is a socially isolated activity so if they're becoming addicted, they're likely to be spending excessive amount of time online alone. Don't be fooled by your child's defense that all they have is their online friends. It is not the same as a personal interaction, and research is beginning to demonstrate this. This is not to say that most children or adolescents who use the Internet are addicted—this is not the case. There are plenty (probably the vast majority) of children who can use the Net in a healthy and productive manner. However, you still may want to monitor what they're doing online.

- *If your child does become exposed to sexually-explicit material, then you should talk about it together with your child.* If it seems they may be developing a problem as a result of viewing such material, or if you're concerned about the degree of their Internet use, you should consider arranging for a consultation with a psychologist or other mental health professional. Preferably with experience in addiction and the Internet, along with appropriate child and family psychology experience.

In some cases the adult Web sites contain information that is so obscene and potentially toxic that people have reported strong negative physiological and psychological reactions to viewing them. There are events on the Internet that can be experienced as traumatic. Such experiences can produce a "traumatic stress response," which is a type of anxiety reaction that can produce nightmares, flashbacks, recurring intrusive thoughts, depression, and more. This traumatic stress reaction is produced when the mind is exposed to something that is very upsetting and is beyond typical human experience.

In some cases this can be the equivalent of being sexually abused, where you are exposed to a sexually traumatic experience without the ability to control its impact or outcome. The Web can produce a similarly powerful impact on a viewer.

You might consider purchasing a second computer that could be dedicated to yours or your children's use. There are many good machines available today at reasonable prices, which may well be worth the peace of mind they bring.

Remember, anything you download from the Internet is usually saved on your hard drive as a file, and sometimes downloads are saved without your even knowing it! Be careful not to save anything you wouldn't want your children to see on the computer or for your children to use. Try to check your hard drive regularly to determine if there is anything saved that might be inappropriate for kids.

Parents should jointly determine a set of values for what is appropriate to have accessible to your child. This includes discussing work-related material that may be sensitive or private as well as other adult-related material.

If you're going to save files or downloads, consider doing so on floppy or other media storage like a zip drive. Some of the newer storage disks can hold large amounts of data, and can be removed from the machine. Many of the newer machines purchased today either come with or can be configured with one of these drives.

Talk to your children. Don't be afraid to ask your child what they're doing online and whom they're talking to. Show interest in their Internet activities, and let them know that there are limits to their use of the Internet. Set up clear rules and guidelines for how and when the Internet will be used in your home and tell them why you're concerned. Obviously, these discussions need to be adjusted for your child's age and computer knowledge, but it's never too early to start developing good habits.

Model good Internet use patterns for your children. Perhaps the best way for your children to learn to use the Internet responsibly is to see how you do so. Children watch everything we do, and they often (if not always) repeat what we do, even if we don't like what we do ourselves!

The good news is that the Internet is a wondrous and powerful educational tool for your children to learn and grow from. The Net can also be entertaining and fun, providing everyone in the family with opportunities to connect with the world's information. There are hundreds of sites devoted to parenting and children, along with various sites devoted to finance, education, healthcare, and consumer issues. The Internet has much to offer you and your children, and with a little caution it can certainly enrich the quality of your family's life. With proper steps to guide and protect your children's use of the Internet, they will be able to enjoy all the benefits while balancing the potential risks.

12

The Future Is the Present That Hasn't Happened Yet

New Uses and Abuses of the Internet

If it can be imagined, it can be possible.

The fact that the Internet is growing so rapidly is not surprising to me. Rather, it seems logical that the Internet would be such a powerful force in the world when you consider the revolutionary change it poses for humanity. The Internet is not simply a new form of communication. Unlike the radio, phonograph, movies, or TV, the Internet is fully interactive. Even the telephone doesn't appear to produce the same accelerated intimacy that can occur online. The Net allows the user to shape the very nature of the communicative experience. It is perhaps the closest analogy to actual human experience which, in part, accounts for its incredible popularity—and addictive potential.

The need to communicate and connect with other people is a part of the primary essence of our humanity. We need to talk to each other. We need to connect. The content of the connection isn't always what's so important; rather it's the process of communicating that gives us our humanness. Even conducting business and commerce is a once-removed excuse to talk. Have you ever wondered why we have so many business meetings? Sure, meetings accomplish a task, but are there not more efficient ways to accomplish this? The answer is yes, but getting something done can be secondary to the process of communicating with each other.

There's Always a Catch . . .

The Internet is in its infancy. What we've seen so far is but a glimpse of the potential of the Internet's influence on our lives. And we've also only seen the beginning of the problems associated with this new technology. Again, this shouldn't surprise us, as all technology has a dark side. The insistence on maintaining the idealistic belief that what we create has to be all good is naive at best, and dangerous at worst. Everything we create has a potential impact on our lives and everything good has to have a *dialectic*, or opposite, position.

The Internet is no exception. With all its present and future greatness, there are many potential problems with the Internet: safety concerns, abuse, workplace issues, child protection, compulsive shopping, gambling, effects on marriage, and Internet addiction are among the areas we can now recognize. None of these problems, however, should dull the shining star of this new technology, but rather should create a new awareness to keep balance in our lives. Technology only serves us if we keep some perspective on how it effects us and, therefore, its ultimate place in our lives.

The Peril and Potential of Cyberliving

Let's take a look at the future changes that are likely to occur with the Internet. I will offer what I believe to be a glimpse into the future of this new medium. I view the changes in the Internet to be particularly exciting. The Net will not only change how we communicate, but also how we are entertained, conduct business, learn, manage finances, use the telephone, and watch TV.

Here is the point in the book where I reveal that I am a true cyberfreak with technophilic tendencies. But I balance this with my real life, I swear! I will try to temper my enthusiasm for technology with the saner side of my personality, as a psychologist practicing in the fields of addictionology, business consulting, and family psychology should.

I expect that the Internet will change the way we live our lives in large ways. The fact that most, if not all, businesses have a Web presence indicates an almost religious faith in this, as yet, unproven technology. Why? The reason is simple. The Internet represents a complete departure from any traditional communications or commerce model previously known. Because of this radical departure, all bets are off, and it's a new game. Businesses have had to virtually reinvent themselves to fit the Internet mode of commerce. Even non-Internet businesses are affected by the psychological shift in business philosophy. The same holds true for the interpersonal side of the Net, where people are treating e-mail and chat rooms like a virtual Mardi Gras, where they can don the cybermask of their choice and be whomever they wish. Although cybersex and online affairs now have digital trails to give away their secrets, new software may even erase the capacity to trace such digital dalliances. It's a whole new game.

There is now more e-mail than paper mail, many times over! E-mail can represent a virtual slot machine, where each time you open a message you experience the excitement of winning a prize! There is an excitement in the adventure and newness of cybercommunication, but I believe a potential loneliness can occur. Aside from chat rooms, e-mail, and the burgeoning e-commerce areas, there are other potential growth areas for this new technology. I will offer here what I see as the future of the Internet (some which has already begun to occur as I write this text). I will also endeavor to plot my view of its potential development. Finally, I will discuss some future problems for individuals and society as we further expand this technology.

How the Net Will Look Over the Next Few Years

- *The faster the better.* Over the next 2–5 years as speed and bandwidth continue to grow, Internet access will begin to achieve an ease of use similar to cable TV.

- *One or two easy ways to do it.* There will be a consolidation of various data transmission systems to one or two standardized methods. Both will provide two-way high-speed data/Internet access and will be affordable. Communications services will be available in service packages, including: Internet access, cable TV, wired telephone (local and long distance), cell/PCS phone, beeper service, and cable/satellite TV. The more communications services you purchase, the cheaper the rate you'll receive from the vendor. Already, numerous companies are positioning themselves to be one of these companies.

- *Wireless communication services will continue to be the fastest growing segment of the telecom and datacom industry.* Prices will continue to drop on wireless services and will shortly approach and surpass the affordability of wired connections. There will be considerable development in satellite, radio, and cellular technologies, to bring the Internet wherever we are. Wireless Internet access is likely to expand over the next few years, and will be the natural outgrowth of our "wired world."

- *The world gets smaller and companies get bigger.* There will be only a few major players in the telecommunications, data, and Internet business and they'll continue to consolidate as the technology and industry mature. Content and distribution partnerships and joint ventures will continue to flourish; several entertainment companies will consume large Internet Service Providers as the market matures. I predict the growth of what I term "edutainment," which seamlessly blends education and entertainment content in one consumable media.

- *Half the homes in the United States will be online within three years (or sooner).* Internet access at home will be on par with the TV, VCR, and telephone. It will be considered essential to have Web access, and will no longer be a novelty. Many products and services will only be accessible on the Net.

- *There are many roads to Rome.* There will be a continual growth of alternate (non-computer) methods of access to the Internet, including: cell/PCS phones, PDAs (personal digital assistants), palmtops, smart wired phones, TV set top boxes, public Internet links, and others. The tool of choice is likely to become a combination cell phone/PDA/Web browser/beeper. It will be completely portable, small, and wireless, and it may soon be as commonplace as the beeper is today!

- *There will be an all-in-one-easy-to-use package.* There will be the development of Integrated Communications Ports in our homes. These will be similar to the portable ones mentioned previously, but will be placed through out your home or business. There will also be public versions available. From these ports you'll be able to run Internet based programs (using Web-based software and your data), send faxes, make video phone calls, check e-mail, and browse the Web. They will be easy, quick, and relatively inexpensive.

- *The PC starts to reach its mature position in the market.* The PC/Mac stand-alone computer will no longer be the sole, nor preferred, mode of access into the Internet. Other portable, cheaper, and simpler units will usurp the use of the PC or Mac for Internet access.

- *Software will be downloadable or be accessible real-time via a Net-based server.* The Internet will become the big server in the sky and will supply software to purchase or lease. Or better yet, you'll simply rent the use of the applications in real-time and store the data on your computer. There are companies that will offer storage of your data on their equipment, which will all be linked via the Internet. This is already happening on a limited scale, but could become a preferred means to manage any amount of data in the future.

- *The Internet will continue to grow the world economy.* E-commerce will continue to grow as it will come to represent a sizable percentage of retail sales. It will also grow in the wholesale and industrial/manufacturing sectors as well. The use of the Internet in business and industry will continue to increase efficiency, and help maintain good profit margins in the economy. Because the Net changes the dynamics of how people interact, it will alter the fundamental structure of how people do businesses and how they view commerce. Our expectations for service and delivery will continue to grow and develop.

- *Shopping will become a whole new game.* Not only will you be able to shop, but also you'll be able to pick from personalized catalogs that are customized to meet your taste and budget, which may be based on previous purchase and buying patterns. Some will even store personal information such as color preferences, sizes, and previous purchases for coordination purposes. Financial data will be more permanently stored, in an encrypted form, and be accessible for any online purchases you make. Weight management and diet plans will be customized and monitored via the Internet as well.

- *The Net will become the preferred modality for purchasing by mail.* Many things will have to happen first. The process of purchasing online needs to be streamlined and made much easier. Right now it's too hard to make purchases online because you have to enter and re-enter so much data. There are attempts at trying to save your financial data, but for the most part these systems aren't viable at this time. Once the Net becomes truly user-friendly, where you can hop online quickly (as quick as turning on the TV or making a phone call), find what you want, and get back off, then shopping will *really* take off. For many items, it's still easier to call a number and place an order by phone, but this is changing fast!

- *Computer and Internet-related software will continue to get better, faster, and cheaper.* Internet technology will really reach the masses when getting online is as easy as flipping on the TV. I predict that within three years or so, we'll have such easy access, although it's questionable whether it will be through stand-alone computers, other Web access systems such as Web TV, or portable wireless devices. Even now many new items are being developed and released as we speak that will *not* have super computing power, but *will* be able to connect to the Internet quickly and efficiently. Processor speed will be of decreasing importance with greater emphasis paid to peripheral speed and efficiency. Peripherals are things like the hard drive, RAM, disc drive, modem, printers, video, and sound.

- *Wires to the world.* High-speed cable modems will continue to grow and expand along with Digital Subscriber Lines (DSL). There is some uncertainty as to which format will win out, but for now it seems likely that both will expand rapidly as the thirst for faster Internet connections continues to grow. Each format has its strengths and weaknesses, but *both* offer far superior speed to present modems.

Future Problems and Abuses

The Internet is here to stay. I have little doubt of that. Every day we hear of a hot new Web site, or the latest Internet IPO. The Internet is being discussed frequently on radio, TV, and is mentioned in almost every magazine and newspaper in some fashion. Numerous major news magazines have often devoted whole issues to some facet of the Internet. All this, and the Internet has only just begun to spin its Web!

No Pain, No Gain

With this growth in Internet technology and business there are bound to be some problems. In the California gold rush of the late 1840s, the sudden growth of population and wealth brought about sanitation problems, disease, pollution, crime, violence, and prostitution. Some things never change. The advent and growth of any new industry brings about some pain with its gain, and the Internet is no exception. There are many negatives that are likely to continue to develop, as well as some potential new ones as well. The following is a partial list of some negative Net-effects.

- *The Net will grow as a problem in the workplace.* As Internet access and speed grows in the workplace, so will the potential for abuse and addiction. In our recent study we found that among Internet addicts, nearly one-third of the time they spent online was at work! This means that nearly 35 percent of potential productivity is virtually lost. Employers will have to do a lot of educating and monitoring if they don't want the Internet to have a negative impact on their bottom line. In addition, there are numerous legal and personnel issues that will need to be addressed in setting and enforcing company Internet policies.

- *Online gambling may become a real public health issue.* If offshore casinos are allowed to continue to offer virtual extensions of their gaming services, people will definitely use and abuse them. The ease of access, instantaneous reinforcement, and anonymity will be very addictive for some people, and there will be many financial hardships as a result. For Internet and gambling addicts this will be a double whammy, as providing easy access to gambling can create significant problems for many people who might otherwise not gamble. The fact that all you have to do is point and click makes it almost too easy, and we may have a whole new generation of virtual gambling addicts.

- *New software that creates the possibility of untraceable and anonymous e-mail traffic can increase the potential for new digital crimes.* We'll continue to struggle with the balance between freedom of speech and the risks caused by a totally anonymous communications medium. There will be ongoing debate regarding accountability and anonymity on the Internet, with some type of regulation a virtual certainty.

- *Children will be at increased risk for exposure to inappropriate material online.* We have not resolved the issue of what to do to protect our children from accessing inappropriate information on the Internet. It's unclear when legislation or industry self-monitoring will occur. Child protection software is available, but not reliable. The best defense is still parental supervision and involvement. Parents will have to continue to check and recheck the parental controls on their browsers to keep up with the new ways that adult Spam sneaks through.

- *Heavy Internet users may find themselves feeling more depressed and socially isolated.* Preliminary research suggests that extended use of the Internet can contribute to depression and social isolation. Remember that anytime you are online you're not doing something else. The Net itself may not be so damaging, but rather, the fact that you may be avoiding other aspects of a healthy and balanced life while online is.
- *The world is becoming too complex and stressful.* There are no simple choices anymore. The increasing reliance on higher technology forces greater levels of stress. When we're available and connected to the world constantly through technology, we remove some of the natural pauses that we need to charge our human batteries. We haven't, in my opinion, begun to address the long-term implications of how this technological stress will affect people's health, relationships, and emotional well-being.
- *Technology can create a more impersonal world.* Although the Internet can foster interpersonal communications, there are risks of increased social isolation that can occur from extended Net use. There's also little long-term evidence to access whether or not Internet-based relationships do as well as more traditional ones, and whether online intimacy is as resilient as its real-time counterpart.
- *Greater Internet use will undoubtedly create more online addicts.* As the Internet continues to expand, with 6 percent of Internet users potentially developing an Internet addiction problem, there will a need for greater education and awareness of Internet-related problems.

- *There are numerous legal issues that remain unresolved regarding the Internet.* Aside from the freedom of speech issue, there are numerous copyright, privacy, and intellectual property concerns. A recent leading issue involves MP3 downloadable music files. With the improvement in search engine efficiency and access speed, the Internet is moving from an information technology, to an entertainment-content technology. The music industry is very concerned about illegitimate access and distribution of copyrighted materials for obvious reasons. It's simply the latest in an ongoing clash between the universal access-minded Internet adherents, and those content developers who have something to protect.

- *Compulsive shopping may become an increasing problem for some Net users.* The increased speed of access, along with anonymity, may increase the potential for compulsive spending. Although this can also occur by shopping in stores and by phone, the Internet's features of disinhibition, ease of access, and twenty-four-hour availability may offer a more potent platform for compulsive shoppers. I believe compulsive e-shopping will likely increase as e-commerce technology improves in speed and efficiency.

- *Computer and Internet based games are clearly addictive.* Just ask any dedicated adult or child and they will tell you of the many virtues of this high-tech pastime. There could be a problem as Web-based games become more prevalent in terms of their easy and inexpensive access. To play Web-based games you don't need any special programs or game players, you simply need a computer (and perhaps a joystick), which put games within the reach of any Web user. Many of these games have violent themes that create further concerns over exposing our children to such intense and realistic material. We have some tough decisions ahead of us.

After reading the previous list, one may conclude that I am anti-technology. I am certainly not antitechnology nor am I anti-Internet. I'm actually quite positive about the future of cyberliving, but I also think we need to understand how our virtual world will affect us as we head into this electronic frontier. It is clear to me that there is much to benefit from this strange new world, as well as a few things to fear. Mostly, however, we need to remain open and learn more about this amazing technology that brings the world home to us. All new advancements carry their price and the Internet is no different. By gaining a better understanding of how we and our world will be affected by the Net, we can better hope to maximize the rich benefit it offers.

Epilogue

My editor told me that I have to wrap up the book and send you, the reader, off with some encouragement. This seems like a good idea, for above all, I want those of you who are being negatively affected in some way by the Internet to be helped by this book. The Internet is a very new technology, and we are just starting to understand the psychosocial implications of this new medium. I received a phone call today from a man who had some significant difficulty in his life, as the result of what he believed was an addiction to the Internet. He began his story by expressing frustration in the lack of knowledge within the healthcare community on this topic, stating that he feels that he's educating his doctors, when it should be the other way around! He is quite correct, as few healthcare practitioners know anything about Internet abuse and addiction.

We know that the Internet is probably here to stay and that it will undoubtedly have a significant impact on our lives, both now and in the future. We also know that we must balance the power and utility of the Net with the need to protect our children. We shouldn't despair, however, for there is such benefit to be found online. With a little care and caution, you can enjoy the Internet without fear of doing any harm. On the other hand, for those of you who feel you've already developed an addiction to the Net, or are abusing it, you can change your situation and do something differently, as you've hopefully discovered by reading this book.

If Your Loved One Is a Nethead

For those of you who are friends or loved ones of Internet addicts you have a tough call ahead of you. It's terribly hard to compete with a computer for time and attention. You must be willing to set boundaries and limits and to stick to your guns with regard to what you expect from your spouse or friend. Do not stand by watching. Express your preferences, and make reasonable demands. Do not give in to the temptation to let the computer win over your real-time importance. Fight for your relationship, and be willing to set limits on what you will tolerate. Offer help and support, but be careful not to offer it unconditionally. All relationships carry a degree of mutual responsibility.

If you have expressed your preferences to your Internet-addicted loved one, and they're still surfing, then you may need to psychologically remove yourself from the situation. Sometimes a support group (similar to Alanon) can be helpful, and there are several available groups online. A list of such groups can be found in the Resources section this book. It is preferable that a support group should be attended in person, especially for the Nethead who has probably become isolated from social interaction. However, for spouses and friends of Internet addicts, the Internet may ironically be an ideal place to gather information and support. These online groups help to teach how not to enable and otherwise indirectly encourage the addictive behavior pattern of use.

Motivated by love and concern, enabling behavior is not easy to address, and can be quite difficult to change. Often, the enabler himself feels addicted to the habit of indirectly supporting the dysfunctional behavior of their spouse or friend. The key is to seek the same support and counsel that I recommend for the addict. Change is difficult enough without trying to do it all alone.

It was my goal in writing this book, that beyond all of the information presented, I have above all offered hope. After all, the only certainty in the world is that change is inevitable, and that we can either embrace it or delay it. I trust this book has helped you in your personal quest to cope with life's inevitable changes and take control of your relationship with the Internet.

Resources

The following Q and A is from a chat with psychologist Dr. David Greenfield on *ABCNEWS.com*, March 29, 1999. In the section after these frequently asked questions, you'll find a list of places you can go for help if you're addicted to the Net. I've also included sites offering Internet tips for you and your kids, as well as sites related to other types of addiction.

The Internet can be entertaining, educational, and even social. You can interact with people around the globe. But its appeal can also lure you away from the real world, hooking you for hour after hour of surfing, chatting, and shopping. How do you know if you're addicted to the Net? In August of 1998, I collaborated with ABCNEWS.com to launch a comprehensive survey on Internet addiction. And now those results are in. The following is a transcript of a live chat on ABCNEWS.com on March 29, 1999, in response to the survey.

Frequently Asked Questions about Internet Addiction

Q: What's the criteria someone should go by to find out if they're addicted?

A: Essentially, if you're spending a lot of time online and it's interfering with your life. That is, if your Internet use is causing difficulty in your life, interfering with work, home, or relationships, then you may have a problem. Consider such questions such as: Are you spending an excessive amount of time online? Are you preoccupied with the Internet? Are you keeping it a secret from people? Do other people think you might have a problem? Do you experience intense intimacy with others while online? Can you not wait to go online or to use the computer? These can all be signs of addiction. However, there's no way to officially diagnose a condition without seeing a professional.

Q: I wonder if my attention span has been influenced by surfing the Net. Recently, I've had trouble concentrating on conversations and comprehending books—I have to reread everything. Can you comment?

A: My sense is that because the Internet is such a powerful multimedia experience, you may become desensitized to less stimulating things, like reading. Attention and concentration can decrease as a result of depression, and there's preliminary evidence to suggest that excessive Internet use can increase depression.

Q: Dr. Greenfield, do you find that people who work on the Internet as part of their daily job become addicted? In other words, is the Internet itself addictive, or does the addiction stem from the person?

A: Good question. There seem to be elements of the Internet that are addictive. However, since only about 6 percent of people that use the Internet become addicted, there probably are contributing factors that are unique to each person.

Q: How does one break the cycle of Net addiction when it's necessary to use the Internet for work?

A: By strictly limiting access to the Internet to single tasks that have to be done. Log off between those essential uses. Let other people know you have a problem, so they can help keep you on track. That may not include your boss. Also, stay away from sites that you find particularly seductive or attractive to you. For many, this often includes sex sites.

Q: How is Internet addiction related to depression?

A: A study that recently came out shows a link between heavy Internet use, social isolation, and depression. This is probably because real-time social interaction is, in my opinion, necessary for healthy psychological functioning. The Internet cannot act as a complete substitute for the real thing. Keep in mind that this is only one study so any conclusions should be tentative.

Q: Do you have any sense for how successful, if at all, relationships have been for people who have met online?

A: I'm not familiar with any studies yet that have looked at the ongoing success of relationships that started on the Internet vs. traditional relationships. I suspect that there are some differences, although we're not sure what they are yet. That's a good idea for a study. There is one difference that we do know: people seem to report experiencing intense intimacy online, more readily than in traditional relationships.

Q: Can you please tell me all the kinds of problems Internet use cause?

A: Internet use in and of itself doesn't cause a problem. It is the combination of heavy Internet use and avoiding other real-life activities important to maintaining a healthy life.

Q: What scientific studies have there been about Internet addiction?

A: There's probably been less than a dozen. Myself, Dr. Kimberly Young, Dr. Orzack, Dr. Al Cooper, and a handful of other people have studied the psychological aspects of Internet use. Because the Internet is so new and changing daily there haven't been many journal articles to date that address the issue of addiction. Internet addiction is only now being recognized as a legitimate area of scientific study.

Q: About what percentage of Internet addiction is pornography related?

A: There's a very high use of pornography among Internet addicts. Sixty-two percent of Internet addicts are logging on to porn sites. However, 46 percent of nonaddicts are also logging on to those sites. But don't forget, two-thirds of the eighteen thousand people we surveyed were men, who tend to access porn sites more regularly. Clearly, an aspect of the addictive nature of the Internet cannot be separated from sexual interest and/or addiction, but I believe there are other aspects of the Internet separate from sexuality that are addictive in and of themselves. [See my response to a question about the similarities between Internet and gambling addictions for more on this.]

Q: I have more of a statement than a question. I spent almost all of my time on the Internet a few years ago. It ruined my marriage. I spent as little time as possible cooking or cleaning, and paid my husband of thirteen years no attention. It can happen. You won't even know it's happening until your husband is gone, your kids are out running around, and you suddenly look up and you're the only one there! I wouldn't wish this on anyone.

A: Your story is not unusual. It reflects the dark side of the Internet that we're only beginning to see.

Q: What concerns you the most about Internet addiction, especially in the future?

A: Very good question. As bandwidth and access speed increase, I think we're going to see an increase in Internet addiction, both among adults and children, and especially in the workplace. In addition, there are numerous freedom of speech issues, as well as new software that's coming out to prevent the traceability of e-mail and Internet communication. This will potentially create new cybercrime opportunities with virtually no means of detection.

Q: Is their a correlation between Internet addiction and gambling addiction?

A: Yes. The initial study done by Dr. Young looked at gambling addiction as a model for Internet addiction, and there seem to be significant similarities. Not the least of which are the loss of recognition of time passing, the feeling of disinhibition, and intensity, along with the negative results of these things on the addicts' lives. My research definition of Internet addiction is also based on the psychiatric definition of compulsive gambling, which I've adapted to Internet use.

Q: Have any of the studies conducted shown underlying reasons or causes for Internet addiction

A: My latest study has looked at the factors I think may be contributing to the addictive nature of the Internet. They include multimedia stimulation, ease of access, twenty-four-hour availability, lack of boundaries, loss of time, disinhibition, stimulating content, among others. What we're not sure about yet is what among these elements are most significant in contributing to addiction.

Q: Where is the line drawn between an enjoyable activity and an addictive behavior?

A: Good question. The line, from my perspective, is when it interferes with your life significantly. If somebody enjoys using the Internet six or eight hours a day and they're still living a healthy and balanced life, it's possible that there's not a problem. However, I'm not sure that someone can spend most of their time online and still have a truly balanced life.

Q: Don't you feel the net just causes new "couch potatoes." I can't see any difference between addicted to TV, video games, or the Net. Are couch potatoes considered addicts?

A: Of course, Internet addicts would be chair potatoes. You're quite right in drawing an analogy between TV and the Internet. I believe there is a similarity between the two mediums. However, the Internet is more potently addictive because of its interactive nature. I do have numerous patients who are significantly affected by the fact that they watch thirty to forty hours of TV a week. The average American watches six and a half hours of TV a day. It's not surprising that one's life can become unbalanced if one is not moving off of the couch or the chair. I have seen numerous marriages affected by the attention they pay to the television and/or the Internet.

Q: Medical literature states that approximately 90 percent of unmarried men masturbate. While two-thirds of your study were men, how many were unmarried? Your study indicates that about 40 percent of "addicted" people masturbate, but only 10 percent of "nonaddicted" people. Could your data be skewed or biased? Could those who are "addicted" simply be younger men?

A: You're quite right in some respects. The survey only asked about masturbating while online, not masturbating in general. The survey certainly is skewed insofar as two-thirds of the respondents were men. Among the women, only 5 percent of the general sample admit to masturbating while online, vs. 17 percent among the men. Among Internet addicts, there is clearly a greater likelihood for men to masturbate as compared to women; however, women are still admitting to this behavior 25 percent of the time.

Q: What are some other strategies my partner and I can consider regarding use and amount of time at the sex sites? If it is an addiction, is zero time at this site the way to break the cycle? Are there any research studies that show the impact on marriages and the use of Internet sex?

A: There are some new study results on cybersex and Internet sexuality that are being released, done by Dr. Alvin Cooper and his colleagues. I recently co-authored a chapter on Internet sexuality in a professional book called *Psychological Perspectives on Human Sexuality*, edited by Muscarella and Szuchman. There are proponents of the Internet who feel that pornography can be a stimulating addition to marriages. If it's not interfering with other aspects of your life or marriage, then I'm not sure there's a problem. Cybersex, however, which is a form of online explicit sexual dialogue, may be viewed as a violation of the marital contract similar to an affair, and this *could* cause problems in a marriage.

     Finally, if you feel you're becoming addicted to these sites, then yes—total abstinence may be required if you're unable to manage your use in a moderate manner.

Q: Is an online discussion on this topic really the best idea?

A: Good question. My research is not about condemning the Internet. I think the Internet has extraordinary uses and possibilities. While my research is about determining the psychological aspects of Internet use and abuse, I view the Internet as a viable tool in both conducting and disseminating information. Any tool, whether it be television, the Internet, etc., can be abused, however.

Q: Can Internet addiction lead to other addictions?

A: We don't know. There appears to be some correlation between Internet addiction and other addictions, but there isn't enough research that I'm aware of to show a definite relationship. We do know, however, that many people who have one addiction frequently have other addictions simultaneously, or may switch the addiction when stopping a previous one. Thirty-three percent of those surveyed were told by *someone they knew* that they had an addiction of some type.

Q: I realize there might be a correlation between pornography and Internet use. I feel that if pornography were less accessible, I might not use my computer as much. Are their any studies that show a connection between addiction and restricting access to pornography?

A: There are no studies at this point. However, for Net addicts who tend to use pornography online excessively, it may be difficult to resume normal Internet use unless they're able to block access to the adult Web sites, which can be very difficult to do. It's too prevalent.

Q: Are you addicted?

A: That's the best question yet. The answer is no, but I certainly could be if I didn't have a strong value on other parts of my life. I do see the power of the Internet. In fact, my interest in this topic came from my own initial reaction to going online. However, you should speak to my wife for the real answer. One other thing: There is a difference between addiction and abuse. I, like many people, have been guilty of abusing the Internet at times.

Q: What about the Internet as an avenue for compulsive shopping and spending? The Net makes it very easy to find and buy things. I can already feel this becoming a problem for myself.

A: This is an excellent question, and I have a chapter in my book, *Virtual Addiction*, about it. You're quite right that the Internet makes it extraordinarily easy to find and buy things. I think this is primarily because of the anonymity and instantaneous gratification that is available when shopping online. You might consider that there are support groups for compulsive shopping and spending that could be useful, whether you're shopping online or in stores. You might want to consider restricting your Internet shopping in attempting to address this.

It's going to become a much bigger problem because, as speed increases, there will be a way to store your financial data in your computer so you won't have to re-enter your info every time; you'll be able to click a button and instantly order. It's going to make the *Home Shopping Network* look like a mom and pop store.

Where to Go for Help

The Web addresses and resources noted in this text were active and relevant at the time of publication. However, due to the rapidly changing Internet and the developing field of Internet research, no guarantees can be made as to the accuracy of the resources noted here. Simply typing in keyword "Internet Addiction" will likely yield the most up-to-date information and potential resources.

Also, please note that no information appearing anywhere in this text constitutes a medical or psychiatric diagnosis or treatment plan. Any information provided is for informational and educational purposes only. If you wish to receive diagnostic or treatment services, please contact a licensed healthcare professional. You may contact Dr. David Greenfield for further information about services available at Psychological Health Associates (www.psychhealthnet.com or www.virtual-addiction.com), or for information about obtaining a referral for professional assistance.

Internet Addiction

Although some of these Web site addresses may change, as this occurs frequently, most are well-established organizations that will most likely keep their Web sites up for a good while still. These addresses were accurate as of July 1999.

Virtual-Addiction.com

An Internet addiction test, news, articles, research information, consultations, media information, and more. This Web site is developed and maintained by Dr. David Greenfield, author of this book and one of the world's leading authorities on Internet addiction and related problems. (860) 233-9772, ext. 14, or (203) 794-1044, ext. 14. http://www.virtual-addiction.com

Dr. Greenfield also maintains a private treatment and corporate/forensic consultation practice at Psychological Health Associates in Connecticut (www.psychhealthnet.com)

Center for Online Addiction

Research, counseling, consultation, and information on online addiction. This site is run by Dr. Kimberly Young. http://netaddiction.com

Caught in the Net, by Dr. Kimberly Young

A book on how to recognize the signs of Internet addiction and a winning strategy for recovery (Wiley and Sons 1998).

Quiz Newsweek.com Extra: Internet Addiction

Interactive quiz to help you decide whether you're spending too much non-work time at the keyboard. http://www.newsweek.com/nwsrv/tnw/today/ex/ex0107_1.htm

Internet Addiction Survey

A survey to assess your Internet addiction level, plus an article on what to do. http://www.stresscure.com/hrn/addiction.html

Internet Anonymous

A list of the most common symptoms of Internet addiction, confessions by addicts, and even a twelve-step self-help program. http://members.aol.com/Iainmacn/addicts/

Internet Behavior Questionnaire and Addiction

Questionnaire and information on Internet behavior and addiction. http://www.ifap.bepr.ethz.ch/~egger/ibq/res.htm

New ERA: Electronic Relationship Addiction Quiz
An online quiz to assess your level of Internet addiction.
http://www.pan-arts.com/era/humor/addiction-quiz.htm

New York Times: Addicted to the Net!
Article on Internet addiction and how it affects people.
http://www.cwrl.utexas.edu/~claire/texts/addiction.html

Spirituality and Cybersex
www.ctaz.com/~firstso/cybersex.htm%3e

Online Support Groups
An Internet Addiction Support Group and a Cyberwidows
Support Group are available. These groups are moderated.
http://www.onelist.com

Josie Levine, Ph.D.
Offers individual and couples counseling for Internet addiction
in San Francisco. (415) 979-3085 or jlev@pobox.com

Patrick Mcginnis, LMHC, CCJAPP
Private practice at the Center for Human Potential located in
Ft. Lauderdale, Florida, specializing in sexual addiction and
co-dependent partners. Recently started Computer and Internet Recovery Support Group. (954) 566-9091.

Proctor Hospital
One of the first clinics in this country to offer Computer/Inter-
net Addiction Recovery Services with both inpatient and out-
patient care as part of the Illinois Institute of Addiction
Recovery program located in Peoria, IL.

You Know You Are Addicted to the Internet When . . .
A collection of signs related to Internet addiction.
http://www.hpc.ntua.gr/~ktroulos/Neat/computer.html

Children and the Internet

The Internet Kids and Family Yellow Pages, by Jean Amour Polly
(Osborne/McGraw-Hill). Thousands of fun Web sites that are
fun and *safe.*　www.netmom.com

Kids Online: Protecting Your Children in Cyberspace, by Donna Rice Hughs (Revell/Baker Book House 1998). This book offers suggestions and parenting resources for protecting your children from the negatives of the Internet. www.protect-kids.com

Enough is Enough
A national, nonprofit organization devoted to protecting children online. 1-888-2-ENOUGH or www.enough.com

America Links Up (ALU)
A coalition of corporate and non-profit organizations that promote Internet safety for children. www.americalinksup.org

Children's Journeys through the Information Age, by Sandra Calvert (McGraw-Hill 1999).

Mental Health and Related Issues

Depression Central
Clearing house of information on depression and various links. www.psycom.net/depression.central.html

Emplyee Assistance Professionals Association
Professional association that deals with Employee Assistance issues. www.eap-association.com

Mental Health Net
Thousands of online mental health resources.
www.cmhc.com

APA Help Center
The consumer resource Web site from The American Psychological Association offering information, resources, and research on a variety of mental health topics.
http://helping.apa.org

Self-Help and Psychology Magazine
A valuable Web-based resource on psychology and self-help issues.   www.shpm.com

Computer Addiction Services at McLean Hospital
This is the first treatment program exclusively devoted to the treatment of computer and Internet addiction problems; Dr. Maressa Hecht Orzack runs the program.
www.computeraddiction.com

Cyberwidows
This site provides information and resources to spouses of Internet addicts.   http://web20.mindlink.net/htc/4_1.html

The Internet Addiction Support Group
To subscribe to electronic mail list, send a message to listserv@netcom.com that reads "subscribe i-a-s-g" in the message area.

National Mental Health Consumers Self-Help Clearinghouse
For individuals interested in starting a local self-help group (either for Internet addicts or support for family members), this site provides information on how to establish a local self-help support group.   www.mhselfhelp.org

Sexual Addiction and Recovery

Sexual Compulsives Anonymous
www.sca-recovery.org

Sexual Recovery Institute
www.sexual/recovery.com

Heart to Heart Counseling Centers
www.sexaddict.com

The Institute of Staged Recovery
www.theinstitute.org/fall4a.htm

Sexaholics Anonymous
www.sa.org

S-Anon
www.sanon.org

San Jose Marital and Sexuality Centre
www.sex-centre.com

Sex Addicts Anonymous
www.sexaa.org

Sex, Lust & Heartache
www.helpvideo.com

Sexual Compulsives Anonymous
www.sca-recovery.org

Sexual Recovery Institute
www.sexualrecovery.com

References

Althauser, D. 1999. *You Can Free Yourself from Alcohol and Drugs*. Oakland: New Harbinger.

Azoulay, J. F. 1999. Online seduction. *Connecticut Family,* March: 14–34.

Bayles, F., and P. O'Driscoll. 1997. Cybercults earn money, recruit on Web. *USA Today*, March: 28–30, 1A–3A.

Brenner, V. 1997. Psychology of computer use XLVII. Parameters of Internet use, abuse, and addiction: The first 90 days of the Internet usage survey. *Psychological Reports*, 80(3):879–882.

Bricking, T. 1997. Internet blamed in arrest for neglect. *The Cincinnatti Enquirer*, June 16: A1–A6.

Burrows, P., and A. Reinhardt. 1999. Beyond the PC. *Business Week*, March 8: 78–88.

Cohen, A. 1999. Cyberspeech on trial. *Time* February 15: 52.

Cooper, A., S. Boies, M. Maheu, and D. Greenfield. In Press. Sexuality and the Internet: The next sexual revolution. In *Psychological*

Perspectives on Human Sexuality: A Research-Based Approach, edited by F. Muscarella, and L. Szuchman. New York: Wiley.

Cooper, Alvin, Coralie Scherer, Sylvain Boies, and Barry Gordon. 1999. Sexuality on the Internet: From sexual exploration to pathological expression. *Professional Psychology: Research and Practice,* 30(2):154-164.

Cooper, A. 1998. They gotta habit. *People,* March 30: 109–112.

CommerceNet. 1999. Cupertino, CA. Internet: www.commercenet. com.

Crockett, R. 1999. A Web that looks like the world. *Business Week,* March 22: 46–47.

Cummings, N. A. 1985. Savvy health care dollars through psychological services.

DeYoung, J. 1998. C'mon, just one more click. *Working Woman,* March, 22:32.

Diagnostic and Statistical Manual of Mental Disorders (DSM-IV). 1996. Washington, DC: American Psychiatric Association.

EAP. 1992. *EAPA: Vital Issues in Employee Assistance* (Stress at home and in the workplace). Employee Assistance Professionals Association..

———. 1992. *EAPA: Vital Issues in Employee Assistance* (utilization and cost benefits). Arlington, VA: Employee Assistance Professionals Association.

Eisenberg, D. 1999. Now it's one big market. *Time,* April 12: 64–66.

Elmer-Dewitt, P. 1995. On a screen near you: Cyberporn. *Time,* July 3: 38–45.

Forcier, A. 1999. Hooked on a feeling: Computer addiction service at McLean's helps break the dependency. *Massachusetts Psychologist,* January: 1–3.

Forrester Research, Inc. 1999. Cambridge, MA. Internet: www. forrester.com

Furchgott, R. 1997. If you like the suit, click here. *Business Week,* November 17: 8.

Greenfield, D. 1999. The nature of Internet addiction: Psychological factors in compulsive Internet use. Paper Presented at 107th American Psychological Association Convention. Boston, MA.

———. 1999. Internet overload. ABCNEWS.com. Moderated chat, March 22.

———. 1997. Crossing the Line—Online. *Self-Help and Psychology Magazine.* World Wide Web (www.shpm.com).

————. 1995. Marital and relationship guidelines for enhancing intimacy. World Wide Web: *psychhealthnet.com*.

Gross, N. 1999. Building global communities. *Business Week,* March 22: 42–43.

Grover, R., A. Reinhardt, and P. Elstrom. 1999. Cable rushes the Net. *Business Week,* April 5: 32–34.

Hester, R., and W. Miller. 1995. *Handbook of Alcoholism Treatment Approaches Effective: Alternatives.* Boston: Allyn and Bacon.

Holstein, W. G., S. Thomas, and F. Vogelstein. 1998. Click 'til you drop. *US News and World Report,* December 7: 42–45.

Jacobson, N. S., and G. Margolin. 1979. *Marital Therapy.* New York: Brunner/Mazel.

Johnson, S. 1999. Web of lies. *The Edmonton Sun,* April 25: 8–9.

Jupiter Communications, Inc. 1999. New York. Internet: www.jup.com

Koerner, B. I. 1999. So that's why they call them "users." *U.S. News and World Report,* March, 22: 62.

Krantz, M. 1998. Click till you drop. *Time,* July 20: 34–41.

Kraut, R., M. Patterson, V. Lundmark, S. Kiesler, T. Mukopadhyay, and W. Scherlis. 1999. Internet paradox: A social technology that reduces social involvement and psychological well-being. *American Psychologist,* 53(9):1017–1031.

Lowinson, J., P. Ruiz, R. Millman, and J. Langrod. 1992. Substance abuse: A comprehensive textbook. Baltimore: Williams and Wilkins.

McClymont, F. 1999. A geek tragedy? *The Independent Magazine,* March 4: 45.

McDonnell Douglas Corporation and Alexander Consulting Group. 1989. EAP cost offset study. Source *EAPA*.

McDonald, D., D. Gordon, and T. Carey. 1996. Surfing the Net to make more. *Money,* November: 120–130.

Millar, H. 1997. For neurosis press enter. *Business Week,* October 27: 163.

Morris, B. 1999. A primal problem emerges from the shadows in a new—and dangerous—corporate environment. *Fortune,* May 10: 66–80.

Nielsen Media, Inc. 1999. New York. Internet: www.nielsenmedia.com.

Okrent, D. 1999. Raising kids online: What can parents do? *Time,* May 10: 38–43.

Penner, N. 1999. Surfing the Internet: Can it be addictive? *Register Report,* Winter: 1–6.

Piller, C. 1999. Seduced by the game: Addicts of online play jeopardize jobs and personal lives. *Los Angeles Times,* May 10: C1-3.

Prochaska, J. O., and C. C. DiClemente. 1986. Toward a comprehensive model of change. In W. R. Miller and N. Heather (Eds.), New York: Plenum Press.

Quittner, J. 1999, Fun with e-mail. *Time,* March 15: 98.

Ramo, J. 1997. How AOL lost the battles but won the war. *Time,* September 22: 46–62.

Remez, M. 1997. Supreme Court ventures into cyberspace. *The Hartford Courant,* March 16: A1–A7.

Schonfeld, E. 1998. Schwab puts it all online. *Fortune,* December 7: 94–112.

Seaman, D. 1998. Hooked online. *Time,* October 12.

Sklaroff, S. 1999. Email Nation. *US News and World Report.* March 22:54–62.

Taylor, C. 1999. Digital dungeons. *Time,* May 3: 50.

Trebilcock, B. 1997. Child molesters on the Internet. *Redbook,* April: 100–138.

Turkle, S. 1995. *Life on the Screen.* New York: Simon & Schuster.

Ullman, J. 1998. Cybersex. *Psychology Today,* October: 29-65.

Van der Leun, G. 1998. The unrepentant voyeur. *Penthouse,* July: 131–133.

Weil, M. M., and L. D. Rosen. 1997. TechnoStress: Coping with technology @ work @ home @ play. New York: John Wiley and Sons.

Weissberg, M. 1983. *Dangerous Secrets: Maladaptive Responses to Stress.* New York: W. W. Norton and Company.

Winters, R. 1999. Modern malt shop. *Time Digital,* May 17: 66.

Wright, R. 1998. Sin in the global village. *Time,* October 19: 130.

Yang, C., R. Siklos, S. Brull, and L. Armstrong. 1999. America Online—and on the air. *Business Week,* May 24: 33.

Young, K. 1998. Caught in the Net. New York: John Wiley and Sons.

———. 1996. Internet Addiction: The emergence of a new clinical disorder. Paper presented at the 105th annual convention of the American Psychological Association Toronto, Ontario, Canada.

About the Author

Dr. David Greenfield is a practicing psychologist and business consultant, with specialties in family psychology, corporate consulting, and addiction treatment. He is founding partner of Psychological Health Associates, LLC, and director of Virtual-Addiction.com. Dr. Greenfield's research and clinical work on Internet addiction has appeared on CNN, ABC News, CBS News, Fox News Network, NBC National News, and in *U.S. News and World Report,* the *L.A. Times, Redbook, Woman's World, USA Today, Kiplingers, Financial Times, PC Computing* and numerous other publications, and he is recognized as one of the world's experts on Internet addiction. He is the author of the largest study on Internet use to date and is on the cutting-edge in understanding how the Internet affects our lives. Dr. Greenfield currently serves as president of the Connecticut Psychological Association, and maintains his consulting practice and home in Connecticut with his wife and two children.

More New Harbinger Titles

INFIDELITY

Step-by-step guidance shows readers how to deal with the shock of discovery, decide what an affair tells them about their marriage, and choose to break up or to rebuild. *Item INFI $13.95*

MAKING THE BIG MOVE

An innovative collection of exercises and practical suggestions help you come to terms with the anxiety of a major relocation and make the transition an opportunity for personal growth. *Item MOVE $13.95*

HEALTHY BABY, TOXIC WORLD

Helps parents understand the threat of common enviromental toxins and take steps to safeguard their child from potentially harmful chemicals. *Item BABY $15.95*

WORKING ANGER

A step-by-step program designed to help anyone who has had trouble dealing with their own anger or other people's anger at work. *Item WA Paperback $12.95*

SEX SMART

"*Sex Smart* is *the* book on everything you probably didn't know about why you turned out the way you did sexually—and what to do about it." —Arnold Lazarus, Ph.D. *Item SESM $14.95*

CLAIMING YOUR CREATIVE SELF

The inspiring stories of thirteen women who were able to keep in touch with their own creative spirit opens the door to new definitions of creativity and to the kinds of transforming ideas that will change your life. *Item CYCS $15.95*

Call **toll-free 1-800-748-6273** to order. Have your Visa or Mastercard number ready. Or send a check for the titles you want to New Harbinger Publications, 5674 Shattuck Avenue, Oakland, CA 94609. Include $3.80 for the first book and 75¢ for each additional book to cover shipping and handling. (California residents please include appropriate sales tax.) Allow four to six weeks for delivery.

Prices subject to change without notice.

Some Other New Harbinger Self-Help Titles

The Self-Esteem Companion, $10.95

The Gay and Lesbian Self-Esteem Book, $13.95

Making the Big Move, $13.95

How to Survive and Thrive in an Empty Nest, $13.95

Living Well with a Hidden Disability, $15.95

Overcoming Repetitive Motion Injuries the Rossiter Way, $15.95

What to Tell the Kids About Your Divorce, $13.95

The Divorce Book, Second Edition, $15.95

Claiming Your Creative Self: True Stories from the Everyday Lives of Women, $15.95

Six Keys to Creating the Life You Desire, $19.95

Taking Control of TMJ, $13.95

What You Need to Know About Alzheimer's, $15.95

Winning Against Relapse: A Workbook of Action Plans for Recurring Health and Emotional Problems, $14.95

Facing 30: Women Talk About Constructing a Real Life and Other Scary Rites of Passage, $12.95

The Worry Control Workbook, $15.95

Wanting What You Have: A Self-Discovery Workbook, $18.95

When Perfect Isn't Good Enough: Strategies for Coping with Perfectionism, $13.95

Earning Your Own Respect: A Handbook of Personal Responsibility, $12.95

High on Stress: A Woman's Guide to Optimizing the Stress in Her Life, $13.95

Infidelity: A Survival Guide, $13.95

Stop Walking on Eggshells, $14.95

Consumer's Guide to Psychiatric Drugs, $16.95

The Fibromyalgia Advocate: Getting the Support You Need to Cope with Fibromyalgia and Myofascial Pain, $18.95

Healing Fear: New Approaches to Overcoming Anxiety, $16.95

Working Anger: Preventing and Resolving Conflict on the Job, $12.95

Sex Smart: How Your Childhood Shaped Your Sexual Life and What to Do About It, $14.95

You Can Free Yourself From Alcohol & Drugs, $13.95

Amongst Ourselves: A Self-Help Guide to Living with Dissociative Identity Disorder, $14.95

Healthy Living with Diabetes, $13.95

Dr. Carl Robinson's Basic Baby Care, $10.95

Better Boundries: Owning and Treasuring Your Life, $13.95

Goodbye Good Girl, $12.95

Fibromyalgia & Chronic Myofascial Pain Syndrome, $19.95

The Depression Workbook: Living With Depression and Manic Depression, $17.95

Self-Esteem, Second Edition, $13.95

Angry All the Time: An Emergency Guide to Anger Control, $12.95

When Anger Hurts, $13.95

Perimenopause, $16.95

The Relaxation & Stress Reduction Workbook, Fourth Edition, $17.95

The Anxiety & Phobia Workbook, Second Edition, $18.95

I Can't Get Over It, A Handbook for Trauma Survivors, Second Edition, $16.95

Messages: The Communication Skills Workbook, Second Edition, $15.95

Thoughts & Feelings, Second Edition, $18.95

Depression: How It Happens, How It's Healed, $14.95

The Deadly Diet, Second Edition, $14.95

The Power of Two, $15.95

Living Without Depression & Manic Depression: A Workbook for Maintaining Mood Stability, $18.95

Couple Skills: Making Your Relationship Work, $14.95

Hypnosis for Change: A Manual of Proven Techniques, Third Edition, $15.95

Letting Go of Anger: The 10 Most Common Anger Styles and What to Do About Them, $12.95

Infidelity: A Survival Guide, $13.95

When Anger Hurts Your Kids, $12.95

Don't Take It Personally, $12.95

The Addiction Workbook, $17.95

Call **toll free, 1-800-748-6273,** or log on to our online bookstore at **www.newharbinger.com** order. Have your Visa or Mastercard number ready. Or send a check for the titles you want New Harbinger Publications, Inc., 5674 Shattuck Ave., Oakland, CA 94609. Include $3.80 for the first book and 75¢ for each additional book, to cover shipping and handling. (California residents please include appropriate sales tax.) Allow two to five weeks for delivery.

Prices subject to change without notice.